KIDSTORY

50 CHILDREN AND YOUNG PEOPLE

WHO SHOOK UP THE WORLD

THERE
IS NO
PLANET B

Atheneum Books for Young Readers

atheneum   NEW YORK LONDON TORONTO SYDNEY NEW DELHI

For all those who've ever felt they shouldn't,
or they couldn't . . . this book's for you.
Remember, you really can!
—T. A.

To my children, Michele and Finley.
Watching you become yourselves is
and has been the most amazing gift.

—S. W.

ATHENEUM BOOKS FOR YOUNG READERS
An imprint of Simon & Schuster Children's Publishing Division
1230 Avenue of the Americas, New York, New York 10020
Text copyright © 2020 by Tom Adams
Illustrations copyright © 2020 by Sarah Walsh
Originally published in Great Britain by Nosy Crow Ltd.
For a full list of photo credits, see page 111.
All rights reserved, including the right of reproduction in whole or in part in any form.
ATHENEUM BOOKS FOR YOUNG READERS is a registered trademark of Simon & Schuster, Inc.
Atheneum logo is a trademark of Simon & Schuster, Inc.
For information about special discounts for bulk purchases, please contact Simon & Schuster
Special Sales at 1-866-506-1949 or business@simonandschuster.com.
The Simon & Schuster Speakers Bureau can bring authors to your live event. For more information
or to book an event, contact the Simon & Schuster Speakers Bureau at 1-866-248-3049
or visit our website at www.simonspeakers.com.
The text for this book was set in Sofia Pro.
The illustrations for this book were rendered in gouache, colored pencil, and Photoshop.
Manufactured in China
1220 SCP
First Atheneum Books for Young Readers Edition March 2021
2 4 6 8 10 9 7 5 3 1
Library of Congress Cataloging-in-Publication Data
Names: Adams, Tom, 1967- author. | Walsh, Sarah, illustrator.
Title: Kidstory : 50 children and young people who shook up the world /
[by Tom Adams ; illustrated by Sarah Walsh].
Other titles: Kid story
Description: First Atheneum Books for Young Readers edition. | New York : Atheneum Books for Young
Readers, 2021. | Title from cover. | Audience: Ages 8 and up | Audience: Grades 2-3 | Summary: "Learn
about fifty amazing kids who changed the world in this beautifully illustrated collection of inspiring short
biographies sure to empower and motivate in equal measure. This volume is the perfect introduction to
just some of the incredible young people from all over the world who have influenced a cultural, political,
or social change throughout history. From Louis Braille to Greta Thunberg, Pelé to Malala Yousafzai,
these activists, inventors, artists, and athletes broke new ground with their passion, courage, and
creativity. Each lavishly illustrated spread features inspiring words from all of these young people and the
true stories behind how their actions and achievements that shook up the world"—Provided by publisher.
Identifiers: LCCN 2020039320 | ISBN 9781534485150 (hardcover) | ISBN 9781534485167 (eBook)
Subjects: LCSH: Children—Biography—Juvenile literature. | Teenagers—Biography—Juvenile literature. |
Biography—Juvenile literature. | Leadership in children—Anecdotes—Juvenile literature. | Creative ability—
Anecdotes—Juvenile literature. | Social action—Anecdotes—Juvenile literature.
Classification: LCC CT107 .A33 2021 | DDC 920.00835—dc23
LC record available at https://lccn.loc.gov/2020039320

CONTENTS

"IF CHILDREN ARE GIVEN AN OPPORTUNITY, THEY FOR SURE CAN CONTRIBUTE TO MAKING THIS WORLD A BETTER PLACE."

—Thandiwe Chama

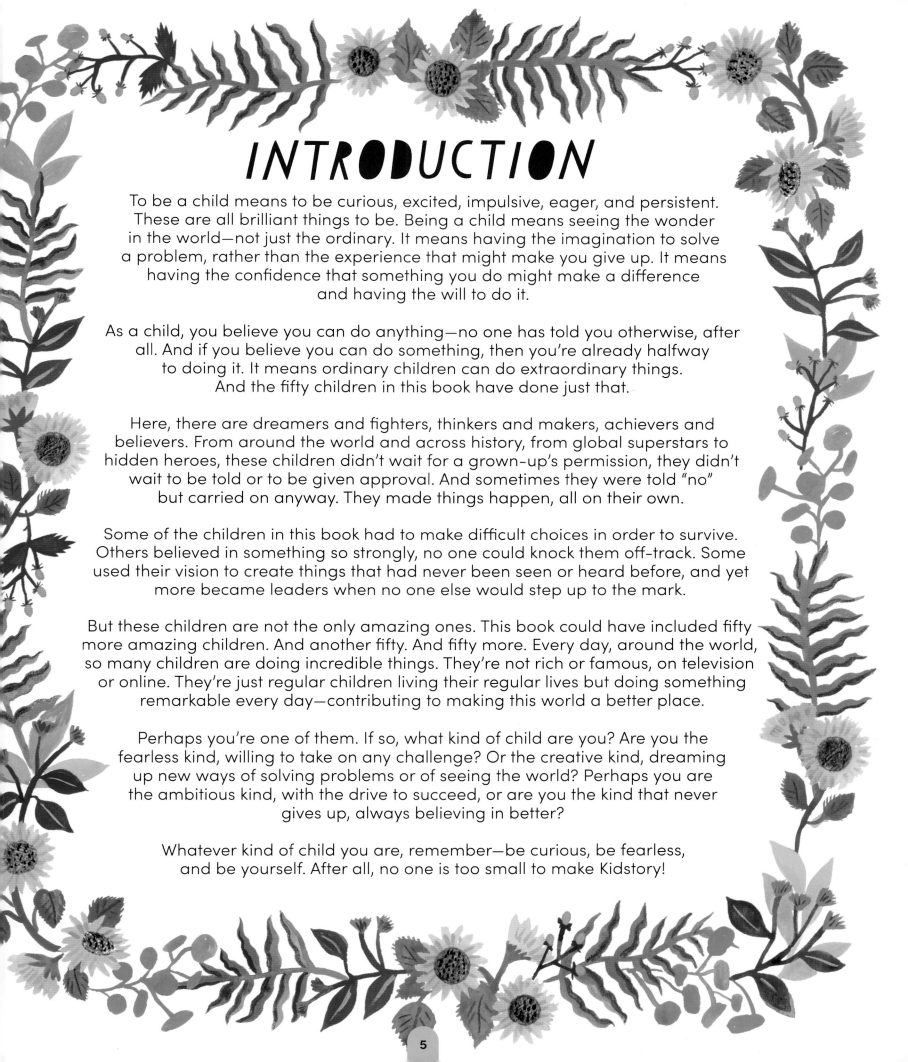

INTRODUCTION

To be a child means to be curious, excited, impulsive, eager, and persistent. These are all brilliant things to be. Being a child means seeing the wonder in the world—not just the ordinary. It means having the imagination to solve a problem, rather than the experience that might make you give up. It means having the confidence that something you do might make a difference and having the will to do it.

As a child, you believe you can do anything—no one has told you otherwise, after all. And if you believe you can do something, then you're already halfway to doing it. It means ordinary children can do extraordinary things. And the fifty children in this book have done just that.

Here, there are dreamers and fighters, thinkers and makers, achievers and believers. From around the world and across history, from global superstars to hidden heroes, these children didn't wait for a grown-up's permission, they didn't wait to be told or to be given approval. And sometimes they were told "no" but carried on anyway. They made things happen, all on their own.

Some of the children in this book had to make difficult choices in order to survive. Others believed in something so strongly, no one could knock them off-track. Some used their vision to create things that had never been seen or heard before, and yet more became leaders when no one else would step up to the mark.

But these children are not the only amazing ones. This book could have included fifty more amazing children. And another fifty. And fifty more. Every day, around the world, so many children are doing incredible things. They're not rich or famous, on television or online. They're just regular children living their regular lives but doing something remarkable every day—contributing to making this world a better place.

Perhaps you're one of them. If so, what kind of child are you? Are you the fearless kind, willing to take on any challenge? Or the creative kind, dreaming up new ways of solving problems or of seeing the world? Perhaps you are the ambitious kind, with the drive to succeed, or are you the kind that never gives up, always believing in better?

Whatever kind of child you are, remember—be curious, be fearless, and be yourself. After all, no one is too small to make Kidstory!

GRETA THUNBERG

THERE IS NO PLANET B

A PLANET IN CRISIS

Greta Thunberg was born in Sweden in 2003. Like many Swedish children, Greta grew up learning the simple ways she could look after the environment: switching off lights, recycling, and putting on a sweater instead of turning up the heat.

Greta was an inquisitive young girl and she wanted to find out more about climate change. What she discovered shocked her. Most scientists believe the world is getting warmer because of the way humans live. Burning fossil fuels, like oil and coal, releases greenhouse gases that are making temperatures rise. If the world doesn't make some big changes very soon, it will spell disaster. The ice caps will melt, sea levels will rise, and there will be regular floods and droughts.

Greta has a very logical mind, which means that if there's a problem, she's good at working out a solution. So she was puzzled when she realized that scientists had already found a simple solution to prevent climate change—stop releasing greenhouse gases. Why, she wondered, if burning coal and oil could cause such harm to the planet, wasn't everybody using renewable energies, like wind or solar power, instead?

> **"YOU SAY YOU LOVE YOUR CHILDREN ABOVE ALL ELSE, AND YET YOU ARE STEALING THEIR FUTURE IN FRONT OF THEIR VERY EYES."**

PERSUADING THE POLITICIANS

Greta realized things had to change, and quickly. She persuaded her family to become even more environmentally friendly. They fitted solar panels, grew their own vegetables, ate less meat, and got an electric car. But one family couldn't save the planet. The whole country had to make a change. She had to force the politicians to act. But what could a fifteen-year-old do?

Then Greta had an idea. She would go on strike! For three weeks, instead of going to school, she sat alone outside the Swedish parliament with her "school strike for climate" sign. She handed out leaflets and talked to passersby to explain what she was doing. Politicians were ignoring climate change and soon the planet and the future of young people would be damaged beyond repair. Greta was challenging the grown-ups to take action.

SCHOOL STRIKE FOR CLIMATE

Slowly people began to take an interest. She appeared on the news and in magazines and was asked to speak at climate conferences. She was very clear about the problem and whose fault it was. The grown-ups were not behaving like grown-ups and it was about time they did. Some people said Greta shouldn't be missing school, but Greta asked why she should go to school to learn facts, when politicians kept ignoring the facts about climate change.

> **" WE CAN'T SAVE THE WORLD BY PLAYING BY THE RULES, BECAUSE THE RULES HAVE TO BE CHANGED. EVERYTHING NEEDS TO CHANGE AND IT HAS TO START TODAY. "**

Young climate activists join Greta to strike against climate change (above) and Greta holding her "school strike for climate" sign (right)

THUNBERG

> **" I AM DOING THIS BECAUSE NOBODY ELSE IS DOING ANYTHING. IT IS MY MORAL RESPONSIBILITY TO DO WHAT I CAN. "**

SHAKING UP THE WORLD

Today Greta is no longer striking alone. She's started a Fridays For Future movement, and children across the world are going on strike every Friday. From Australia to Uganda, Brazil to Canada, children are protesting each week, demanding the people in charge start doing something serious about climate change. Alongside these weekly strikes, Greta has started organizing much bigger Global Climate Strikes every few months, where children don't just strike, but take part in demonstrations, rallies, and protests. On one Friday in September 2019, over four million people in 150 countries showed their support for Greta's campaign.

Greta has won many awards, including the International Children's Peace Prize. She's even been nominated for a Nobel Prize. But what is more important to her is to keep the strikes going to increase the pressure on rich countries until they start seriously reducing their greenhouse gas emissions. With more and more children supporting her across the world, it looks like one schoolgirl really could be the person to save the planet.

WILLIAM KAMKWAMBA

Malawian inventor who harnessed the power of the wind

GOING HUNGRY

A farmer working in a maize field in Malawi, just like the one William worked in with his father

William Kamkwamba was born in Malawi in Africa in 1987, one of seven children. His parents were farmers and, like many in Malawi, they grew a crop called maize. When William wasn't helping his dad on the farm, he was hard at work in school, where he enjoyed lessons and was a good pupil.

In 2001, Malawi suffered a dreadful famine, when the maize crop failed to grow and there wasn't enough food for everyone. William's family only had enough for one meal a day and William and his six sisters were always very hungry. They had no spare maize to sell, so they didn't have enough money to pay for William to go to school anymore.

William really wanted to keep learning, though, and he would visit the local library to read the books there. He liked science and one book in particular caught his eye. *Using Energy* was all about physics. It was written in English, which William didn't understand, but there were pictures, and these helped him figure out what the book was about.

William was fascinated by a page that showed how a windmill could turn wind power into useful energy like electricity, to power lamps or pump water. William's home didn't have any electricity, so he started planning how he might build his own windmill. At first, his mother thought he was crazy.

TURNING JUNK INTO POWER

William visited his local junkyard and found a few things he thought would be useful—a big old fan that was once part of a tractor engine, a broken bicycle, a dynamo used to power a bicycle lamp, and lots and lots of wood.

After some failed attempts and lots of hammering and fastening, William's windmill soon began to take shape. His tractor fan sat on top of a huge wooden tower and turned when the wind blew. This turning caused the bicycle wheel to spin around, which then powered the dynamo. The dynamo transformed all of this movement into electricity, which ran in wires down the tower right into William's house.

> **66** TRUST YOURSELF AND BELIEVE. WHATEVER HAPPENS, DON'T GIVE UP. **99**

WILLIAM KAMKWAMBA

With the first big gust of wind, the light bulbs William had connected flickered to life. Now William's family had electricity! They could power four bulbs and a couple of radios. When his neighbors heard what he had done, a line started forming at his house because everyone wanted to charge their mobile phones!

With one windmill built, William started on another—bigger and better than the first. It was powerful enough to pump water across the farm to spray on his father's maize. Soon, journalists heard of this ingenious young boy and started writing articles about him. Before long, he was being flown around the world to give talks to other young people. He had never left his village before—now he was crossing the globe, inspiring others!

> " I WENT TO SLEEP DREAMING OF MALAWI, AND ALL THE THINGS MADE POSSIBLE WHEN YOUR DREAMS ARE POWERED BY YOUR HEART. "

William's parents, Trywell and Agnes, stand outside their home lit by William's windmill (top) and William talking about his invention on American television in 2009 (bottom)

SHAKING UP THE WORLD

William was offered a place at a college in America to study engineering, and since then he's gone from strength to strength. He wants to improve life in rural Malawi and has raised money to help build classrooms and provide books. But he also wants to find more ways that natural power can help. The new classrooms are fitted with solar panels to convert light from the hot Malawi sun to electricity, so students can study after dark. And William has set up a system called a biomass converter, which turns cow manure into cooking gas, and fertilizer for the fields. Nothing is wasted!

From a junkyard windmill to biomass converters, William is slowly but surely improving the lives of not only his family, but many others in Malawi.

RUTH LAWRENCE

Math genius who broke university records

$$AREA = \tfrac{1}{2}\, ab \sin C$$

$$area = \tfrac{1}{2} \times b$$
$$\times height$$

$$= \sqrt{s(s-a)(s-b)}$$
$$\text{where } s = \tfrac{a+}{2}$$

A GIFT FOR MATH

Ruth Lawrence was born in Brighton, England, in 1971, the daughter of two computer specialists, Harry and Sylvia. Even as a toddler, Ruth showed a gift for math. She used to climb up and down the stairs, counting each step as she went. Her father believed that the best way to learn was to find things out yourself, so he always encouraged Ruth to ask questions and explore the world around her.

Eventually Ruth was old enough to go to school. Her father hadn't enjoyed school much . . . he felt that he hadn't learned as much as he could have. He believed part of the problem was that learning in a big class of children was too difficult.

$$C = \sqrt{a^2 + }$$
$$b = \sqrt{c^2 - a^2}$$
$$a = \sqrt{c^2 - b^2}$$
$$B(x_2, x)$$
$$A(x, y)$$

He didn't want the same thing to happen to his daughter. Instead, Harry gave up his job and became Ruth's teacher. From the age of five, she was taught everything at home . . . in a class of just one! Ruth was a very quick learner. It was clear that she was a natural at math, but to make the most of her talent, she had to work very hard. In her father's eyes, playing with her friends would only have distracted her. So instead, when she wasn't studying, Ruth would play the piano or watch television.

> **66** ENJOY THE SUBJECT, THE BEAUTY OF THE SUBJECT. MY FATHER BROUGHT ME UP WITH MATHS ALWAYS AROUND ME. I ALWAYS THOUGHT IT WAS VERY BEAUTIFUL. **99**

TOP OF THE CLASS

By the time Ruth was nine, she was ready to take her math O Level. This was a big exam taken by almost every child across the country. The only difference was most children were sixteen when they took the test—seven years older than Ruth! Not only was she the youngest person ever to take the O Level, she got an A for it too, the best grade.

Ruth arriving for her first day at university on a tandem bicycle with her father, Harry

Later that same year, Ruth sat her math A Level, an exam normally taken by eighteen-year-olds. It was no surprise when she got another A grade. Then she took the entrance exam to study math at Oxford University, one of the best universities in the world. Five hundred and thirty students took the test and nine-year-old Ruth came top of them all! The time had come for her to move to Oxford to continue her learning. Here she could learn far more than her father could ever teach her.

66 I WAS ALWAYS EAGER TO LEARN MORE. 99

Because she was so young, Ruth's father moved with her, and they went to all her classes together. They were often seen cycling from lesson to lesson and lecture to lecture on a tandem bike. Ruth worked very hard and even ended up correcting her teachers' work: in one class, while explaining a problem, a senior math tutor covered the blackboard in complicated mathematics. As the rest of the class struggled to keep up with the symbols and squiggles on the board, Ruth called out, "You've made a mistake." And he had!

RUTH LAWRENCE

St Hugh's College in Oxford University

Most students spend three years at university, but Ruth finished her course in just two. In her final exams she received a "starred first" and became the youngest person ever to receive a first-class degree: she scored enough marks to achieve the top grade twice over!

SHAKING UP THE WORLD

After her math degree, Ruth studied for a second degree—this time in physics. Then she took another degree in math at Oxford. By nineteen, and with three degrees, she was teaching other mathematicians at Harvard University in the US, while doing her own mathematical research in her spare time.

Today, Ruth is still a brilliant mathematician. She lives in Israel with her husband and four children. When she's not teaching, Ruth investigates a complicated area of math known as "knot theory." She is still learning and challenging herself, asking questions and exploring the world around her.

MARY ANNING

Fossil hunter who helped us understand life on Earth

LIFE ON THE BEACH

Mary Anning was born in 1799 in Lyme Regis, a small seaside town in Dorset, England. Her family was very poor even though her father, Richard, worked hard as a carpenter and tried to make money any way he could.

The pebbly beach at Lyme Regis was famous for the strange stones that could be found there. These stones, known as snakestones, devil's toenails, or petrified serpents, were washed up by the sea or would fall from the crumbling cliffs that stretched along the shore. Some scientists wondered if these snakestones were the remains of dead animals that had roamed the Earth long ago. Today, we know that these scientists were right, and these stones were fossils.

Mary and her father hunted for fossils and seashells, which they sold to vacationers as souvenirs. Scientists, trying to understand what these strange objects were, would visit and discuss the stones with Mary.

> **" SHE SELLS SEASHELLS ON THE SEASHORE. "**
>
> *Song by Terry Sullivan said to be inspired by Mary Anning*

FINDING FOSSILS

When Mary was just eleven, her father died. Now fossil hunting became even more important for Mary and her brother, Joseph, as it was a way for them to make enough money to feed their family. One day, Joseph discovered what looked like the skull of an ancient giant crocodile on the shore. Somehow the skull had become separated from the skeleton. Mary was determined to find the rest of the mysterious animal's bones. She spent days and days scouring the beach, hunting for anything that might be part of the strange creature.

Lyme Regis on the Jurassic Coast in Dorset, where Mary did most of her fossil hunting

Finally, she spotted it, high in the cliff face. With the help of some local workmen, she managed to remove the sixteen-foot-long fossilized skeleton from the rocks. It was clear it wasn't a crocodile. But what was it? And why was it on Lyme Regis beach?

Fossil experts believed Mary had discovered the bones of an extinct creature, which means a type of animal that is no longer alive today. They called it an ichthyosaur, meaning "fish lizard," because it looked like a strange mix of the two. It was sold to a local collector for a huge sum of money and was eventually put on display in the Natural History Museum in London, England, where it can still be seen today.

Mary's ichthyosaur fossil in the Natural History Museum in London, England

Mary also found the fossils of ancient plants, like ferns, which still grow today

❝THIS YOUNG WOMAN IS SO THOROUGHLY ACQUAINTED WITH THE SCIENCE THAT THE MOMENT SHE FINDS ANY BONES SHE KNOWS TO WHAT TRIBE THEY BELONG.❞

Lady Harriet Silvester

SHAKING UP THE WORLD

As Mary discovered more and more fossils, she also began to learn about the history of the Earth. Comparing the hundreds of fossils that she'd found to animals that were still alive, she began to understand how life on our planet had changed over millions of years. When she realized the small black lumps she occasionally uncovered alongside the bones were fossilized poo, it meant she was able to find out what these ancient animals ate, too!

Mary soon became an expert in finding fossilized animals and plants, so that paleontologists (or scientists who study fossils) could investigate her findings. She was the first person to find the fossils of a plesiosaur, a finned underwater reptile that lived at the same time as the dinosaurs, and a pterosaur, a flying reptile. The fascinating remains that Mary uncovered challenged the Bible's traditional creation story and helped scientists understand how old our planet was, how the continents had changed over time, and how life had developed over millions of years.

Mary died in 1847, aged only forty-seven. She is buried at the church in Lyme Regis, close to the beaches and cliffs she knew so well. Although when she was alive she received little thanks for her discoveries, today we are aware of the hugely important contribution she made to science and the understanding of our planet.

MARY ANNING

ANN MAKOSINSKI

Young inventor who turned heat into electricity

STRANGE TOYS

Ann Makosinski was born in Canada in 1997. Some people might think her childhood was rather unusual because, growing up, instead of traditional toys she was given cardboard boxes, the insides of old computers, and other items of household junk to play with. That wasn't all. Ann's mom and dad didn't let her play video games and she never had a smartphone. It meant that Ann had to find other ways to keep herself entertained.

Luckily, she had her imagination, and armed with this and a glue gun, she used her piles of junk to build things. Then she'd dream up pretend jobs for her magnificent creations to work on. These first "inventions" didn't really do anything, but she loved the process of putting together something new. As well as sticking things together, Ann loved to take things apart and whenever her parents were throwing something away, like a broken computer, printer, or kitchen mixer, she'd get out her screwdriver. She didn't understand how these machines worked but was curious to discover what was inside them.

66 ANYONE CAN BE AN INVENTOR. 99

Her parents could see how much she loved science, so when she was ten, they suggested she enter a science fair—a competition where children research the science behind something and present their discoveries. For Ann's first investigation, she did experiments to find out which laundry detergent cleaned clothes the best.

LIGHT-BULB MOMENT

Over the next few years, Ann entered more and more science fairs. She loved trying to solve a problem using her science know-how and was always on the lookout for things she could explore. Entering the Google Science Fair in 2013, she found a great problem to investigate. Ann had been chatting on the phone to a friend who lived in the Philippines. Her friend explained why she hadn't done very well on her exams: the electricity supply to her home wasn't very reliable, which meant she often didn't have any electric lights once it got dark. Without lights, Ann's friend couldn't do her homework.

66 IT'S ABOUT TAKING THAT CREATIVE, CRAZY IDEA YOU'VE GOT AND NOT BEING AFRAID TO FOLLOW IT THROUGH. 99

This got Ann thinking. Was there anything she could invent that could help her friend? A cheap and easy way to provide light? She knew light and heat were both kinds of energy, and so she wondered if she could turn heat from our bodies into light. She tinkered with the problem and carried out some experiments before she came up with a new invention: one that really did work! Ann's flashlight created light without batteries. The Hollow Flashlight uses just the heat of your hand to power it.

Ann's invention won her the top prize at the Science Fair in the 15–16 age category, and a flashlight manufacturer thought her idea was so good, they wanted to make the flashlight and sell it around the world!

" JUST LOOK AROUND YOU AND FIND A PROBLEM. WHEN YOU FIND SOMETHING THAT YOU WANT TO FIX AND IT HAS A PERSONAL CONNECTION TO YOU, IT MAKES YOU MUCH MORE MOTIVATED TO ACTUALLY WORK ON IT. "

ANDINI "ANN" MAKOSINSKI

Ann winning a Green Award (above) and giving a talk at the Greentech Festival in 2019, the first festival to celebrate green technology and sustainability (left)

SHAKING UP THE WORLD

Ann started looking for other hot things that might be able to generate electricity and soon she had invented the eDrink—a cup that uses the heat of a coffee to charge a smartphone. This invention won her the *Popular Science* Young Inventor of the Year Award in 2016.

Today, Ann is at college studying English literature and drama, not science as you might expect. She believes the best inventors are good at science but are also creative—Leonardo da Vinci, who painted the *Mona Lisa*, invented all kinds of extraordinary machines and Albert Einstein, a mathematical genius, was also a gifted violinist. Ann is still young, but she keeps inventing incredible things in her spare time: she's also developed toys that teach children about renewable energy. Who knows what extraordinary things she may yet invent to make the world a better place?

BLAISE PASCAL

A wood engraving of
Blaise as a young child

SKETCHING SHAPES

Blaise Pascal was born in 1623 in Clermont-Ferrand in France. His father, Étienne, was a brilliant mathematician and one of the cleverest men in the country. So instead of sending him to school, his father decided to teach Blaise at home. He started with Latin and Greek lessons because he was worried that if he started with math, Blaise would enjoy it so much, he would ignore his other subjects. But Blaise had other ideas.

He was an inquisitive young boy and could often be found sitting in his room drawing shapes on the floor with a piece of charcoal. He'd figure out how to calculate the angles in a triangle or the length of a side . . . for fun!

Without even realizing it, Blaise was teaching himself geometry—the mathematics of shapes and lines. One day, his father discovered him in his room, charcoal in hand. Instead of being angry at the triangles and squares scribbled across the floor, Étienne burst out laughing and realized it was time to start the math lessons!

> **KIND WORDS DO NOT COST MUCH. YET THEY ACCOMPLISH MUCH.**

LEARNING THROUGH EXPERIMENTS

Blaise was always asking questions about the world and his father encouraged him to find out the answers by doing experiments himself. One evening at dinner, when his metal knife tapped his drinking glass, Blaise was surprised by the sound. He experimented, tapping on different materials and silencing the sound with his hand. It got him thinking about how sound works and led him to write his first scientific paper at the age of eleven.

> ❝ SINCE WE CANNOT KNOW ALL THERE IS TO BE KNOWN ABOUT ANYTHING, WE OUGHT TO KNOW A LITTLE ABOUT EVERYTHING. ❞

BLAISE PASCAL

Blaise was growing up at a time when great thinkers were beginning to explore how the world worked in a scientific way. He realized experiments could be used to prove whether an idea was right or wrong and started investigating air and pressure. By doing some clever experiments, Blaise discovered that facts about pressure had been misunderstood for centuries. He went on to explore pressure in liquids and invented a way of using this pressure to lift heavy weights, something we still use in things today, from car brakes to diggers.

When Blaise was sixteen, he wrote another paper all about the mathematics of cones. It was so complicated that one French mathematician didn't believe Blaise could have written it, but he had! The math he explored was so useful, architects and designers still use his ideas today.

> ❝ MAN'S GREATNESS LIES IN HIS POWER OF THOUGHT. ❞

When he was given a complicated puzzle by a friend, he developed a whole new type of math to solve it. What if two people are tossing a coin to see who tosses ten heads first? If, after a number of flips, one player has five heads and the other has six, how likely is it that the player with five heads will win? Blaise worked out a way to explain this with numbers and, in doing so, created the math of probability—predicting the chance of something happening or not. Today, we use probability in everything from weather forecasting to building computer games.

The inside of Blaise's Pascaline mechanical calculator (above) and plans for his incredible invention (left)

SHAKING UP THE WORLD

Blaise even went on to invent the first mechanical calculator . . . while he was still a teenager. His father had to add up lots of numbers in his job as the king's tax collector, so Blaise put his brilliant mind to the problem and came up with the Pascaline—a metal contraption the size of a shoebox that could add and subtract numbers. Blaise called his calculator the *Machine à penser* or "Thinking Machine" and he made over fifty of them in ten years.

Blaise died at the age of thirty-nine, but he had such a big effect on science and math that his name is still found in textbooks today—he has had a unit of pressure, a computer programming language, and several mathematical and scientific laws named after him.

RICHARD TURERE

A MAASAI COWHERD

Richard was born in Kenya in 2000, close to the country's capital, Nairobi. As a boy, he helped his father look after the cattle on their family farm. But this wasn't always as simple as it sounds.

The family live in a national park that is home to rhinos, buffalo, leopards, elephants, lions, and more. But while tourists want to get up close to the wonderful wildlife, Richard didn't. He belongs to the Maasai, a tribe that has lived in the wilderness of Kenya for centuries. They are a traditional warrior people and want to keep their land and belongings safe.

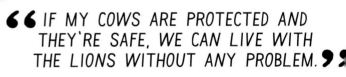

> **IF MY COWS ARE PROTECTED AND THEY'RE SAFE, WE CAN LIVE WITH THE LIONS WITHOUT ANY PROBLEM.**

Wild animals would roam Richard's farm at night and, in the morning, he would often find that one of his cows had been attacked by lions. Some weeks he could even lose nine cows! Some members of the Maasai hunted lions to protect their cows, but lions are in danger of extinction in Kenya, which means there aren't many left in the wild. Although they could cause trouble, Richard didn't want to see all the lions killed. He wondered if there was a way humans and lions could live alongside each other.

So, one night, Richard lit small fires around the cowshed to scare the lions away. It didn't work. Next, he made a scarecrow from old clothes stuffed with hay. With a hat on top, it looked a little like a person from a distance. The following morning, no cows had been hurt. But the next night the lions attacked again. A scarecrow might fool a crow, but lions are clever cats!

RICHARD'S BRIGHT IDEA

One evening, he was checking whether all the cows were safely in the cowshed when he realized his flickering flashlight was scaring the lions. He wondered, could he find a way of using light to make the lions think he was still walking around?

Richard got straight to work. He'd once taken apart his mother's new radio to see if he could rebuild it, so he used the skills he'd learned. He connected an old car battery, some flashlight bulbs, and a switch mechanism from an old motorbike. Adding some solar panels to charge up the battery through the day, Richard strung his lamps around the cowshed.

RICHARD TURERE

" I LOVE TECHNOLOGY, USING MY HANDS AND BEING PRACTICAL. IT'S WHAT I LOVE DOING AND IT KEEPS ME GOING. "

Richard attaching his lion lights invention to a fence close to his home (above) and a cowherd at nightfall in Kenya (left)

That night, the lights around the shed flashed on and off, making it look as if Richard was walking around. And the next morning? No sign of lions. Or the morning after, or the morning after that. Richard's "lion lights" had done the job—while he was asleep in bed! Without complicated equipment or expensive electronics, Richard had protected all the animals, and that meant other farmers could do the same.

SHAKING UP THE WORLD

The lion lights worked so well, soon they were being used across Kenya, not just to stop lions, but elephants, hyenas, and leopards, too. It meant humans could live alongside the amazing Kenyan wildlife more safely, and just two years after the lights had been invented, 750 other farms were already using them.

When one of Kenya's best schools heard of his invention, they offered Richard a place—something a Maasai cowherd could usually only dream of. Today, they're spreading the word about Richard's lion lights and he's busy working on his next invention: a new type of electric fence that he hopes will keep his animals even safer.

" ONE YEAR AGO I WAS JUST A BOY HERDING MY FATHER'S COWS. NOW I WANT TO BE AN ENGINEER AND PILOT. "

BOYAN SLAT

Inventor with a big idea to clean up the oceans

BRAIN WAVE ON THE BEACH

Boyan Slat was born in 1994 in Delft, in the Netherlands. As a little boy, he loved building things. At the age of two, he designed and made his own wooden chair when he couldn't find one small enough to fit him, and he went on to put up his own tree house and zip line in his garden.

But he wasn't afraid to think big, either. At school, when he learned how to build rockets powered by water pressure in science class, he invented a way of launching lots of them at the same time. He even broke the Guinness World Record for launching the most water rockets all at once—213!

When Boyan was sixteen, he went on vacation to Greece and had an idea that would change his life. One day, he went diving in the sea. Instead of discovering a magical underwater world, he saw masses of floating plastic bags and bottles. The sea was just a garbage dump.

Boyan realized the plastic was dangerous to all the fish and other sea creatures. They could easily get tangled up in it, or even try to eat the plastic and die. And because most plastic doesn't rot . . . the bottles and bags he'd seen on his dive could still be there in hundreds of years' time.

So, how could Boyan make a difference? It would never work to collect the plastic piece by piece. The oceans are far too big and the garbage is far too spread out. But then he had a brain wave. He would build something that would travel the oceans automatically, using wind and wave power to pick up the plastic.

> **" I'M AN OBSESSIVE AND I LIKE IT. I GET AN IDEA AND I STICK TO IT. "**

A huge pile of plastic washed up on a beach in the Hawaiian Islands (left) and Boyan at the Ocean Cleanup office in 2014 (above)

PICKING UP PLASTIC

Ocean currents constantly move the waters in the seas around the world. Garbage gets carried by these currents but ends up gathering together in a few calm spots on the planet, a bit like all the garbage in your bedroom ending up under your bed. The Great Pacific Garbage Patch is one such spot—it's a massive stretch of ocean three times the size of France and it contains around 176 million pounds of plastic garbage. That's around 250 pieces for every person on the planet! And because plastic takes so long to break up, it's getting bigger every year.

❝ WHEN PEOPLE SAY SOMETHING IS IMPOSSIBLE, I LIKE TO PROVE THEM WRONG. ❞

Boyan's System 001 was launched from San Francisco, collecting plastic waste in the Great Pacific Garbage Patch between California and Hawaii

BOYAN SLAT

Boyan came up with the idea of an enormous floating barrier that could collect garbage from the Great Pacific Garbage Patch. The barrier could drift around the ocean, powered by wind and waves, scooping up plastic as it moved. Once the barrier had picked up enough plastic, it could be collected by a ship and taken to be recycled.

❝ THE HARDEST THING ABOUT ENGINEERING IS THAT THERE ARE THOUSANDS OF THINGS THAT COULD GO WRONG AND YOU NEED ONLY ONE ISSUE FOR IT NOT TO WORK. ❞

SHAKING UP THE WORLD

There was only one way Boyan was going to find out if his idea would work, and that was to try it out. In 2013, he founded Ocean Cleanup and, together with scientists and researchers, he began to spread the word about his plan. Finally, with enough money raised, he built a test version of his invention and in December 2018, a 2000-foot-long barrier called System 001 was launched into the Pacific Ocean.

It was a success . . . mostly. It soon began trapping floating plastic, however, it didn't work perfectly straightaway. But Boyan did not give up on his ocean cleanup. One year later, it started successfully picking up plastic and soon he hopes to build a fleet of sixty even bigger barriers. In five years, he believes his ambitious invention can reduce the size of the Great Pacific Garbage Patch by half, cleaning up the seas and saving a huge amount of marine life.

REYHAN JAMALOVA

Inventor who discovered a way to turn rain into electricity

BRAIN POWER TO RAIN POWER

Reyhan Jamalova was born in 2002 in northern Azerbaijan. Her parents, Rauf and Ulduz, were very proud when she achieved good grades in her lessons and was accepted by the best school in the area. There, she worked hard, and especially loved her science classes. On the weekends, she would often watch television documentaries about science and discuss them with her father.

It was during one of these conversations that Reyhan and her father started talking about renewable energies—energy generated by wind or wave power or the sun. They couldn't understand why no one had yet tried to generate electricity from rainfall. It got Reyhan thinking.

Every falling raindrop has energy, but this energy is lost once it hits the earth. If a raindrop could be caught before it hit the ground, and its energy somehow converted into electricity, it could provide a clean, renewable, and useful source of power. And while one raindrop falling only has a tiny amount of energy, a whole tropical monsoon is something quite different. Reyhan began to wonder: Could a home be powered by electricity from rainstorms?

CREATING GREEN ELECTRICITY

Fifteen-year-old Reyhan and her friend started crunching the numbers using all their science know-how to try to solve the problem. They calculated how many raindrops would be required to power a single light bulb and then started designing a device that could do the job.

After four months of hard work, they began building their prototype. They called the machine Rainergy and the thirty-feet-high contraption was made up of four separate parts. There was a rainwater collector that caught the raindrops high off the ground and led them to a storage tank. When the water was released from the tank, it ran down to the ground, turning a paddle in a generator. This turning movement generated electricity, much like a dynamo on a bicycle lamp. Finally, this electricity was stored in a battery to be used when needed.

Reyhan hopes that one day Rainergy can be used to light up entire cities, in Azerbaijan and around the world

66 YOU MIGHT NOT BE ABLE TO CHANGE THE ENTIRE WORLD, BUT AT LEAST BY YOUR WORK, YOU CAN CHANGE A SMALL PART OF IT FOR SOMEONE. **99**

REYHAN JAMALOVA

> **"IN THE FUTURE, I WANT TO BE AN ASTROPHYSICIST AND I DREAM OF BECOMING THE NOBEL PRIZE LAUREATE."**

It was a simple design, and when Rainergy was built, it worked straightaway, generating enough electricity to power a number of lamps! Even better, there was no pollution and no greenhouse gases created. This was clean, green electricity.

In 2017, Reyhan entered her invention into a European competition for new green technology ideas—Climate Launchpad. She was the youngest person ever to enter and Rainergy won a prize for being the "best startup." Reyhan then spent time improving her design so that it could generate even more power, before showing it to the world at the Global Entrepreneurship Summit in India.

SHAKING UP THE WORLD

With her motto, "Light up one house at a time," now Reyhan is busy developing the Rainergy equipment. She wants to turn the prototype she built at school into something that can be used by homes and families around the world to provide useful, cheap, green power. Her achievement is so impressive, she made it onto a list of the thirty most promising young entrepreneurs and inventors in the manufacturing and energy industry—the first person from Azerbaijan ever to do so.

> **"OUR FUTURE WILL BE BUILT ON GREEN, SUSTAINABLE, AND RENEWABLE ENERGY."**

23

JORDAN CASEY

Computer whiz and chart-topping game creator

AN EYE FOR BUSINESS

Jordan Casey was born in Waterford, Ireland, in 2000. Like many youngsters, he was always trying to earn extra pocket money, but not all of his moneymaking schemes worked out. He often sold his old toys to make some cash, but once ended up selling his brother's toys by mistake! And another time he managed to persuade his friends to pay him for karate lessons, even though he knew nothing about the sport!

JORDAN CASEY

PENGUINS AND PIXELS

What Jordan did know about, though, was computer games. He liked to play a game called *Club Penguin*, where he controlled a penguin having adventures in a virtual world. Millions of people played the game and many players kept Internet diaries, or blogs, about their gaming. Jordan didn't know how to create an online blog, so he persuaded his grandmother to buy him a book about computer programming.

> **❝ CODING CAN BE REALLY INTIMIDATING WHEN YOU FIRST LOOK AT IT, SO YOU HAVE TO BREAK IT DOWN, AND START TO LEARN THE BASIC LANGUAGE. ❞**

Jordan spent evening after evening in his bedroom teaching himself how to program. His parents thought he had been playing games, so they were surprised, and impressed, when he revealed his blog. And they weren't the only ones. It was so interesting and well-designed, soon thousands of *Club Penguin* fans were visiting his site. So, now that he understood how to program computers—he could do it well and enjoyed it—he looked for a way it could earn him some money!

Jordan soon decided to create his own video game. *Alien Ball vs Humans* was a simple game about aliens invading Earth and when he got it working, he sent it straight to Apple, one of the biggest computer companies in the world.

Jordan still had to attend school while he created his own video games in his spare time

Before he knew it, it was on sale around the globe, and at twelve he became the youngest game developer in Europe. His game even topped the charts in Ireland. Following this success, Jordan built more games and useful apps too. He founded a gaming company, Casey Games, and started looking for problems in everyday life that could be solved with a cleverly written computer program.

When his teacher lost her book with all her students' details, he realized he'd found his next project. The book contained everything the teacher needed to know about her class—names, test scores, exam results, attendance records, and so on. Jordan developed an app called *TeachWare* that stored all this information on the Internet, so it could never be lost again.

"YOU CAN BE SO CREATIVE WITH IT. YOU CAN IMAGINE SOMETHING AND DO ANYTHING WITH PROGRAMMING."

Jordan aged fifteen at home in his bedroom in Waterford, Ireland

SHAKING UP THE WORLD

Jordan kept developing programs. In 2016, he created *KidsCode*—a virtual world that teaches computer coding as you play games and do puzzles online—while juggling schoolwork, hanging out with his friends, and running his businesses. And today, life is getting busier and busier as technology companies like Apple and Google have asked him to give motivational talks to their employees.

Jordan's advice for others wanting to build their own businesses is to start young and follow your dream. It's never been easier to learn something new, thanks to online videos that can teach you almost anything!

"THE POSSIBILITIES ON THE INTERNET AND THE AMOUNT WE CAN LEARN . . . FOR FREE MOST OF THE TIME ON THE INTERNET, IS HUGE."

STEVIE WONDER

One of the greatest singer-songwriters of all time

BLIND AT BIRTH

Stevland Judkins was born in 1950 near Detroit, Michigan. He was a premature baby, which means he was born too early, and he needed to be looked after in a hospital to survive. Because Stevie was so tiny, he was given extra oxygen to help him grow, but this also damaged his eyesight and turned little Stevie blind.

Growing up, even though Stevie couldn't see, his brothers and sisters taught him to climb trees and ride a bike, but it soon became clear that his greatest love was music. It was no surprise—all of his family loved music too. His mother, Lula, listened to songs on the radio all day, dancing in the kitchen as she prepared meals for the family. His father, Calvin, bought Stevie a set of bongo drums before he could even walk, and Stevie was soon singing in the church gospel choir.

❝ WE ALL HAVE ABILITY. THE DIFFERENCE IS HOW WE USE IT. ❞

As he got older, Stevie managed to build quite a collection of musical instruments. Friends and family saw that he had talent, as he bashed out rhythms on pots and pans, so they did what they could to help. He was given a piano by a neighbor and at the age of seven, he learned to play it almost immediately. Soon after, he was given a drum kit and a harmonica. Stevie played and played and played, mastering the instruments almost overnight!

STEVLAND HARDAWAY JUDKINS

Stevie aged 13 playing the Super Chromonica, a special kind of harmonica

When Stevie was eight, his mother took him to a music festival. As bands performed, Stevie stood right by the stage, letting the sounds wash over him. One group noticed the little blind boy, lost in the music, and called him onto the stage. When he revealed he could play the drums, they invited him to join in. Stevie got behind the kit and started beating out a rhythm. He loved the feeling of playing in front of an audience and the applause at the end gave him such a buzz.

BIG BREAK

Stevie was growing up during an exciting time for music and Detroit was right at the heart of it. A man called Berry Gordy had started a music company, the Motown Record Corporation, which created a new pop-soul sound, known around the world as Motown. Stevie managed to get an audition with Gordy, who was blown away by his performance and signed him up on the spot. He even came up with his stage name: the eleven-year-old musician was such a little wonder, it had to be Little Stevie Wonder.

Stevie (front row, center) with the Tamla-Motown tour group, including some of the most popular acts of the day like The Supremes and Smokey Robinson

Stevie made a couple of records with Gordy, but he really came alive when he was performing onstage. In 1962, he went on tour across America with other Motown bands and Stevie was the star of the show. The audiences loved him and he loved the cheering crowds—more than once he had to be pulled offstage to give others a turn. One night in Chicago, his live performance was recorded, and it was released soon after. This became Stevie's first hit record. *Recorded Live: The Twelve-Year-Old Genius* shot up the American Billboard Charts, reaching the number one spot. It made him the youngest artist ever to top the chart!

> **JUST BECAUSE A MAN LACKS THE USE OF HIS EYES, DOESN'T MEAN HE LACKS VISION.**

SHAKING UP THE WORLD

As Stevie got older, he soon dropped the "Little" from his name and started to develop his own unique sound. He mixed together gospel music, rock and roll, jazz, and African rhythms in a way no one had done before. He also kept searching for new sounds with electronic instruments, which went on to inspire other musicians.

As his songwriting developed, Stevie produced hit after hit, with songs like "Superstition," "Sir Duke," and "Living for the City" becoming classics, still loved today. Since then Stevie has won countless awards for his music and has sold over 150 million records—quite a little wonder!

Stevie's star on the Walk of Fame in Hollywood

WOLFGANG AMADEUS MOZART

One of the greatest composers of all time

A MUSICAL HOME

Wolfgang Amadeus Mozart was born in 1756 in the city of Salzburg, which is now part of Austria. His father, Leopold, worked as a composer—somebody who writes music—for one of the most important men in the area, the prince-archbishop of Salzburg.

Music was a big part of Wolfgang's early life and he and his sister, Maria Anna, played instruments and wrote their own pieces from a young age. When he was just three, Wolfgang started to learn tunes on the harpsichord, a piano-like instrument with a keyboard. By four, he could play the violin and would perform pieces composed by his father. By five, he was writing his own music.

> **❝ IF ONLY THE WHOLE WORLD COULD FEEL THE POWER OF HARMONY. ❞**

Wolfgang playing music at home with his sister, Maria Anna, and their father, Leopold

Leopold knew his son had a very special talent and felt it was his duty to develop this rare gift. He supported Wolfgang in any way he could, teaching him, playing him as much music as possible, and encouraging him to write his own pieces. As the young Mozart composed at the harpsichord, his father would scribble down the notes, or score, so his creations could be shared with the world.

THE GRAND TOUR

In 1763, Leopold took Wolfgang, along with his sister, on a grand tour of the great musical cities of Europe. He wanted people to hear Wolfgang play, but he also wanted Wolfgang to hear other composers' music so he could learn from them. They visited Munich, Brussels, Frankfurt, Paris, London, Amsterdam, Lyon, Zurich, and more, before returning to Salzburg three years later. On his travels, Mozart performed in front of royalty, in palace courts, grand concert halls, churches, and cathedrals. Many people flocked to hear the young boy play and they were amazed at how talented he was. He could even play beautifully when blindfolded!

Mozart met many of the most famous composers of the day and studied the pieces they wrote. He could hear how each composer created moods in their music in different ways, combining instruments or patterns of notes to make the listener happy, sad, excited, or tense. Mozart took all these different styles, added his own ideas, and used them to create his own new music. It was while he was on the grand tour that, at the age of eight, he wrote his first symphony—a musical composition for a full orchestra.

Quite brilliantly, Mozart didn't need an instrument to compose music . . . he could hear the notes in his head and write them down. He revealed this exceptional gift when, at the age of fourteen, he visited the Sistine Chapel, the home of the pope in Rome, Italy. He heard the choir there sing a beautiful but very complex piece of music. After the performance, he wrote down the whole score entirely from memory! Mozart even went back to the chapel the following day to listen again, just to correct a handful of mistakes he knew he had made.

❝ I PAY NO ATTENTION WHATSOEVER TO ANYBODY'S PRAISE OR BLAME. I SIMPLY FOLLOW MY OWN FEELINGS. ❞

WOLFGANG AMADEUS MOZART

Wolfgang (right) composed one of his earliest pieces when he was just five years old (above), which had to be written down for him by his father, Leopold, as he couldn't write yet!

RG

SHAKING UP THE WORLD

By the age of fifteen, Mozart had written over eighteen symphonies, along with violin sonatas, piano concertos, and operas. As he got older, he wrote extraordinary pieces of music and, while he is called a genius, he worked incredibly hard writing and rewriting pieces to get them as perfect as they could be. Today, over 250 years later, his music is still loved by millions around the world. When he died tragically young, aged just thirty-five, Mozart had composed over 600 pieces of music, including some of the most celebrated in history. He was considered the greatest composer of his day, but today, it is clear he is one of the greatest composers that ever lived.

EMMA WATSON

Harry Potter star who fights for equal rights across the world

A DREAM COMES TRUE

Emma Watson was born in Paris, France, in April 1990 but spent most of her childhood living in Oxford, England. As a little girl, she loved being in front of an audience—school plays, debating society, reciting poems, anything where she could stand up and perform! It was no surprise when she joined the local drama school.

Another thing Emma loved was Harry Potter books. Emma's father would read them to her at bedtime, and when she was old enough, she read them herself. She loved the character Hermione Granger, who was clever, courageous, and loyal. When she learned there were plans to make films of the books, she was desperate to be in them—and, of course, she wanted to play Hermione.

Her mother took her along to the audition and it went well. Little did she know she would need to audition seven more times before the part was hers! Between each one, she would wait for the telephone to ring, desperate for the producers to call with good news. After the eighth audition, she was in.

> 66 YOUNG GIRLS ARE TOLD YOU HAVE TO BE THE DELICATE PRINCESS. HERMIONE TAUGHT THEM THAT YOU CAN BE THE WARRIOR. 99

Emma starred in all eight of the Harry Potter films, from the ages of 10 to 19

MAKING HER MARK

Emma had a great time acting in the film and, just like Hermione in the books, she wanted to be the best she could be. She learned all her lines carefully, and to make sure she knew exactly when she was meant to say them, she learned Harry's and Ron's lines too.

When the first Harry Potter film was released, audiences thought Emma was brilliant as Hermione. She went on to play Hermione in the next seven films and, at one point, she became Hollywood's highest paid female star. She won many awards and, in 2007, she did what all the top film stars do—left her hand- and footprints (and wand print!) in cement on the Hollywood Walk of Fame. Eventually, after ten years of hard work but lots of fun along the way, the Harry Potter films came to an end.

But as if starring in some of the most popular films ever made wasn't enough, Emma has also designed clothes for an environmentally-friendly clothing company, worked as a model, studied English literature in college, and has even become a fully qualified yoga teacher!

Emma playing Hermione Granger, aged eleven, in *Harry Potter and the Chamber of Secrets* (top) and, aged sixteen, in *Harry Potter and the Order of the Phoenix* (bottom)

> **I'VE ALWAYS BEEN LIKE THAT; I GIVE 100 PERCENT. I CAN'T DO IT ANY OTHER WAY.**

SHAKING UP THE WORLD

For years, Emma had used her fame to highlight inequalities around the world, especially how girls in many countries are unable to go to school. Then, in 2014 the United Nations got in touch with her. The UN is an international association of countries that works to improve conditions for people everywhere. Their HeForShe campaign called for men and women to be treated equally and the UN wanted Emma to help spread the message.

In her first speech, Emma spoke about being called "bossy" because she liked things done her own way. Often, if a boy behaves the same way, he is called "assertive." Being assertive is seen as good, but being bossy is bad and that didn't seem very fair to Emma. Similarly, while it's seen as acceptable for girls to cry if they get upset, boys are meant to "man up." These are simple, everyday examples of the way boys and girls are sometimes treated differently, and Emma wanted this to change.

Today, Emma continues to campaign for equality, which she juggles with all her other interests. She still acts, recently starring as Belle in *Beauty and the Beast* and Meg March in *Little Women*. She's gone from child star to UN ambassador, so whatever's next, it's clear that Emma will make herself heard.

Emma on a talk show discussing her role as UN Women Goodwill Ambassador

> **GIRLS SHOULD NEVER BE AFRAID TO BE SMART.**

EMMA CHARLOTTE DUERRE WATSON

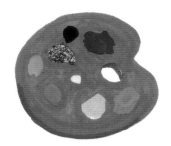

PABLO PICASSO

PENCILS, PAPER, AND PIGEONS

Pablo Diego José Francisco de Paula Juan Nepomuceno Crispín Crispiniano María Remedios de la Santísima Trinidad Ruiz Picasso, or Pablo Picasso for short, was born in 1881 in Málaga in the south of Spain. His father, José, was an artist, and it was José who first encouraged Pablo's interest in art as a child. Pablo used to sit for hours with his pencils and paper, sketching the pigeons in the town square by his home.

Pablo and his father loved watching bullfighting, a national sport in Spain at the time. A bullfighter, or matador, would challenge a bull in front of cheering crowds, making it angry by poking it with sharp spikes. When the bull charged, the bullfighter would dance out of the way, swirling his blood-red cape.

Pablo loved the sights and sounds—the elegance of the matador, the strength of the bull, the excitement of the fight—and he painted what he saw. His early works, like *Le Picador* painted at the age of nine, were good, but not extraordinary. They only hinted at the talent to be revealed.

❝ I PAINT OBJECTS AS I THINK THEM, NOT AS I SEE THEM. ❞

GOING HIS OWN WAY

As Pablo got older, his family moved around Spain while his father taught art in schools across the country. When José wasn't teaching, he would paint pictures to sell and he soon got Pablo helping him in his artist's studio. By the time Pablo was thirteen, José believed his son had become a better artist than he was.

As a pupil at the Barcelona School of Fine Arts, Pablo attended lessons to learn different art styles and techniques, but the better he got, the less he listened to his teachers. Instead, he preferred to paint how he wanted to.

Pablo is named after a long list of saints and close relatives

❝ BAD ARTISTS COPY. GOOD ARTISTS STEAL. ❞

However, by the age of fourteen, Pablo was clearly so talented he was moved up to the senior art classes. His painting showed skill and vision way beyond his years. *First Communion* and *Science and Charity*, both painted when he was fifteen, are paintings with a sense of shape and depth. Pablo used light and shade so skillfully it made the images appear real and solid.

SHAKING UP THE WORLD

But Pablo didn't just want to create pictures that looked real. He wanted his paintings to tell stories and reveal his feelings—what he loved, what he hated, or even what he was scared of. He took ideas from African, Roman, and Greek art, and kept adapting his style of painting to find new ways to express himself. He was an innovator and creator, perhaps best known for starting the cubist movement. Cubism was a new way of painting that showed everyday objects as a collection of simple, flat shapes on a page. It made artists, and audiences, look at the world from different perspectives, or angles, not just from one viewpoint. Pablo also experimented with surrealism—a way of showing thoughts and feelings through painting imagined worlds and objects.

66 THE WORLD TODAY DOESN'T MAKE SENSE, SO WHY SHOULD I PAINT PICTURES THAT DO? 99

PABLO PICASSO

Pablo's *Guernica* on display in the Queen Sofía national art museum, in Madrid, Spain

As Pablo got older, many of his paintings had the power to shock. Audiences would gasp when they saw some of his work for the first time. He created influential images about important subjects, like war or love, and he used strange colors to paint contorted figures and impossible faces. His approach changed painting, and painters, forever.

Picasso died in 1973. He was ninety-one. Over the years, he created thousands of paintings, sculptures, and illustrations. He became one of the most successful and well-known artists of the twentieth century. But it was his spirit and desire to paint the way he wanted, without a care for what others thought, that singled him out as a true creative genius.

BJÖRK

DARING TO BE DIFFERENT

Björk Guðmundsdóttir was born in 1965 in Reykjavík, Iceland. Her name means "birch," a common type of tree in the Icelandic countryside. She was a very musical little girl: by five she was learning the flute and oboe and only needed to hear a song once to be able to sing it.

Björk's parents separated when she was young, so she spent time at both her mother's and father's houses. They liked very different kinds of music—her father liked classical, and her mother liked rock and pop. It meant she grew up listening to a wide range of music. Sometimes Björk's mother would take her into the wilderness to get closer to nature. They climbed mountains, experienced the ice, hot springs, and geysers that made Iceland such a unique place to live, and listened to the extraordinary sounds these natural phenomena made.

Björk released her first solo album at age eleven and received her first Grammy nomination for *Debut*.

> **I'M INFLUENCED BY EVERYTHING. BY BOOKS, BY THE WEATHER, BY THE WATER, BY MY SHOES, IF THEY'RE COMFORTABLE OR NOT. EVERYTHING.**

As a child, Björk stood out from the crowd, partly because she looked so striking—and partly because she liked to do strange things occasionally. One day, she turned up at school wearing her grandfather's clothes. Another time, she didn't wear any clothes at all, just a duvet cover with little holes cut out for her head and arms. It got her noticed!

A FIRST ALBUM

One day at school, Björk's teacher made a recording of her singing a pop song. It was so good she sent it to Iceland's only radio station. Someone from a record company heard the song and promptly offered her the chance to make a record. She recorded *Björk*, her first album, when she was just eleven years old!

The album was a mix of traditional Icelandic songs and pop songs and it went platinum in Iceland, which means it sold over 10,000 copies. Now Björk really had the music bug. With the money she earned from the album, she bought a piano and started to write songs and look for bands to play in.

Over the next few years, Björk recorded albums with lots of different groups playing all kinds of music, from punk to experimental jazz. She looked for ways to make her music and style as unusual as possible—at one point she dyed her hair orange and shaved off her eyebrows! When she sang, she would shriek and howl, but these weren't the only strange noises she turned into songs. Her grandfather's snoring became the beat to one track, and the sound of a popcorn machine making popcorn became the rhythm to another. Clearly, Björk wanted to get the pop into her pop music!

" SINGING IS LIKE A CELEBRATION OF OXYGEN. "

BJÖRK GUÐMUNDSDÓTTIR

By the time she was twenty, Björk was in a band called the Sugarcubes and their records started selling around the world. Newspapers and magazines were fascinated by Björk's quirky looks and a voice that could change in a moment from a little girl's whisper into a wild animal's roar.

Björk famously wore a dress shaped like a swan to an award ceremony (right) and was always very creative on photo shoots (below)

SHAKING UP THE WORLD

When the Sugarcubes split up, Björk became a solo performer, and her album *Debut* was released in 1993. Since then, she has sold millions of records around the world, but more than that she has changed what it means to be a pop star. The skills she learned in childhood shaped the musician she is today. She writes and performs her songs but also controls how they are recorded and how they sound. She combines her musical creativity with work in films, art, fashion, and technology like no other performer.

" I SOMETIMES FALL INTO THE TRAP OF DOING WHAT I THINK I SHOULD BE DOING RATHER THAN WHAT I WANT TO BE DOING. "

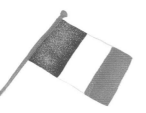

LOUIS BRAILLE

A TRAGIC ACCIDENT

Louis Braille was born in 1809 in Coupvray, a small town near Paris, France. His father made saddles and other riding equipment for horses, and when Louis was little, he loved to try to copy everything his father did.

One day, Louis crept into his father's workshop and grabbed a scrap of leather and a sharp saddler's knife. He started to punch holes in the leather but, unfortunately, Louis's hand slipped and the knife went into his eye. Sadly, the eye could not be saved. Even worse, it became infected, and within a year both eyes were so badly damaged that by the age of five Louis was completely blind.

> 66 WE DO NOT NEED PITY, NOR DO WE NEED TO BE REMINDED WE ARE VULNERABLE. WE MUST BE TREATED AS EQUALS. 99

In the early 1800s, most blind people had no choice but to beg to survive. Louis's family knew it would be almost impossible for him to learn to read and write, and so it would be very difficult to find work in the future. Even so, Louis's parents wanted the best for their son, so they sent him to school just like his brother and sisters and encouraged him to become as independent as possible.

LANGUAGE OF DOTS

In 1819, Louis was selected for a special school in Paris: the National Institute for Blind Children. It was the first school of its kind in the world, but it was a tough place to grow up. Housed inside an old prison, the school was cold and damp, pupils were not given enough to eat, and the teachers could sometimes be unkind.

The school's founder, Valentin Haüy, had worked out a way of making books that blind people could read. Instead of letters printed on the paper, letters were pressed into the paper, creating a raised letter shape. By running a hand across a page, a person could feel the letters and read the words. Unfortunately, it was a complicated and expensive way of making books, so the school only had a small collection for the blind pupils to read. However, while reading these books, Louis realized something special: it was possible to read, not using the eyes, but using another sense, touch.

> 66 ACCESS TO COMMUNICATION IN THE WIDEST SENSE IS ACCESS TO KNOWLEDGE. 99

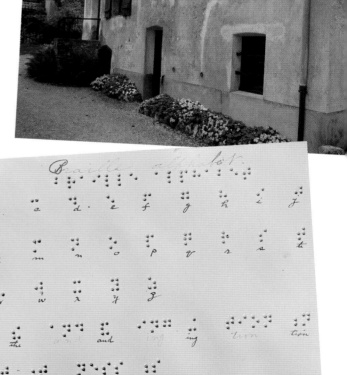

Louis's home in Coupvray, France (top) and the incredible reading and writing system Louis created as a child (bottom)

One day, a French army general visited the school to give a talk about "night writing." The general revealed how, using a code of twelve raised dots and dashes punched into paper, soldiers could read with their fingers in the dark. This got Louis thinking.

He set to work simplifying the army's idea, creating letters out of combinations of just six dots. All together, Louis worked out 63 different dot combinations—enough for numbers and mathematical and punctuation symbols too. Using just six dots meant a symbol was small enough to be read by the touch of a single fingertip, making understanding easier and reading quicker. By 1824, at the age of fifteen, Louis had developed a fully working system.

LOUIS

SHAKING UP THE WORLD

Louis went on to become a teacher at the institute, encouraging the pupils to use his system of dots, known as Braille. But although it meant the boys and girls at the school could read, and so enjoy stories and learn about the world, it took some time before Braille spread worldwide.

Nowadays, Braille isn't only found in books. You might notice the little dots on signs, buttons, and packaging. It's also used in many different languages around the world. Braille is even keeping up with technology as new systems have been developed to help people communicate online without needing print.

This is all thanks to Louis and his bright idea. The system he invented 200 years ago has gone on to help millions of blind people read and write—something that was simply unimaginable before. He proved that, with the motivation and enough determination, he could change the way blind people experienced the world forever.

LOUIS BRAILLE

CLARA SCHUMANN

Celebrated German pianist and composer

PRACTICE MAKES PERFECT

Clara Josephine Wieck was born in 1819 in Leipzig, Germany. Her father, Friedrich, was a piano teacher and decided, even before she was born, that she was going to become a brilliant pianist. Luckily, when Clara started to learn the piano at age five, it was obvious she had a natural talent.

As well as the piano, Clara had lessons in violin, singing, and composing music. This meant she didn't have much time to play with other children. When she wasn't practicing the piano, she was being taken to concerts to listen to other musicians perform. Before each performance, Clara studied the music to make sure she learned something from each one.

CLARA JOSEPHINE WIECK

66 UNDER HER FINGERS THE PIANO TAKES ON COLOR AND LIFE. 99

Tutor of the Duke of Weimar after hearing Clara play

TAKING TO THE STAGE

But all the practice paid off. In November 1830, at the age of eleven, Clara gave a solo performance onstage at the famous Gewandhaus, a grand concert hall in Leipzig. In those days, almost all musical recitals were performed by men. Women sometimes sang—because their voices could reach higher notes than a man's—but it was rare to see women play instruments in public, and even rarer to see an eleven-year-old girl at the piano! Clara broke the mold.

But for Clara to really make it big, she had to be a success in Paris. The French capital was where musicians went to become stars and all the big names were performing there. Clara was determined to prove herself, and in November 1831 she set out for the city with her father.

At the time, the only way to travel around Europe was by horse-drawn coach along bumpy roads. The journey was slow and very uncomfortable. They stopped at towns and cities on the way, where Friedrich would organize concerts for Clara to play at. Everywhere she performed, she received glowing reviews.

"CLARA PLAYED LIKE A GOD WITH UNPRECEDENTED APPLAUSE AND UNANIMOUS BRAVOS."

Her father after a concert in Magdeburg

A beautiful hand-painted portrait of Clara

Finally, three months after leaving Leipzig, Clara arrived in Paris. It was a different world. She discovered new music, new manners, and new fashions. She went shopping for the most fashionable fancy white dresses and met the pop stars of the day, composers like Felix Mendelssohn and Niccolò Paganini. She performed night after night in people's homes and there was a buzz about the gifted young pianist from Germany who played with such skill and sensitivity. Clara went on to perform in sell-out concerts across Europe as a teenager and into her adulthood. She was a sensation.

Clara with her husband, Robert Schumann, painted in 1847

When Clara was twenty, she fell in love and married the composer Robert Schumann, one of her father's students who she had known for many years. In the 1800s, women usually stopped working once they were married, but not Clara. She continued to play concerts and compose her own music. Clara also inspired her husband to write some of his greatest work, which she then performed across Europe.

SHAKING UP THE WORLD

Together, Clara and Robert had eight children but, sadly, Robert became unwell and died when he was only forty-four. Once again, Clara broke the mold. Widows were supposed to stay at home and look after their families. But Clara wasn't ready to give up doing what she loved. Instead, she continued to juggle looking after her children with performing—both Robert's music and her own. In a time when girls and women were under pressure to behave a certain way, Clara spent a lifetime doing what she enjoyed—an extraordinary achievement from an extraordinarily talented woman.

SKYLER GREY

TRAGIC BEGINNINGS

Skyler Grey was born in Los Angeles, California, in 2000. Sadly, when he was just two years old, his mother was killed in a tragic accident. It was left to his father, Holman, to bring Skyler up alone.

As a way of coping with the trauma of losing his mother, Skyler was encouraged to paint and draw. Sometimes people find it helpful to show how they are feeling with pictures instead of words, and this art therapy helped Skyler understand his emotions. The more Skyler painted—and he painted a lot—the more impressive his pictures became. He was always asking for more pens and paper, and even sitting in a movie theater he'd be scribbling away. Soon, Holman realized art wasn't just helping Skyler cope with losing his mother, it was turning him into an artist.

HOW TO GET NOTICED

But Skyler's natural talent wasn't too surprising. He came from a very creative family. His father was a rapper and a poet, his mother wrote plays, and his grandfather was an artist too. Creativity was clearly in his blood and Skyler's father encouraged it any way he could. They would watch television shows about artists, go to exhibitions together, and even hunt out street art and graffiti across Los Angeles so Skyler could soak up every influence he could.

Soon, Skyler began to develop his own distinctive painting style. He would take an image everyone recognizes, like a cartoon character or fashion label logo, and surround it with wild, chaotic designs, layers and layers of paint, different textures, and plenty of color. There are so many layers in his pictures—the more you look, the more you see.

> ❝ IF YOU ARE FORTUNATE ENOUGH TO HAVE A MOTHER IN YOUR LIFE, KISS, HUG, AND THANK HER. ❞

Skyler's father used to show him documentaries as a small child to introduce him to all different kinds of art

Skyler and his father, Holman, preparing his work at the Art Basel art fair in Miami, Florida

This new style of art got him noticed, but Skyler wanted to create a real splash in the art world. He'd seen how the pop artist Andy Warhol became world famous by producing paintings of celebrities like Marilyn Monroe and Elvis Presley. He thought he could do the same so, when he was eleven, he created a series of images of pop star Amy Winehouse painted to look like the British queen, complete with crown and cape.

> ❝ I LIKE TO MAKE PEOPLE HAPPY WHEN THEY LOOK AT MY ARTWORK. ❞

These paintings were a huge success. An art gallery in Los Angeles saw one and immediately offered to put it on sale. Within hours, a collector in Switzerland had snapped it up. Skyler's career had begun! By the age of thirteen, he had work shown in galleries around the world and, at the opening of his first solo exhibition, 800 people came to see his collection.

> ❝ I WAS PUT ON THIS EARTH TO CREATE. ❞

SKYLER GREY

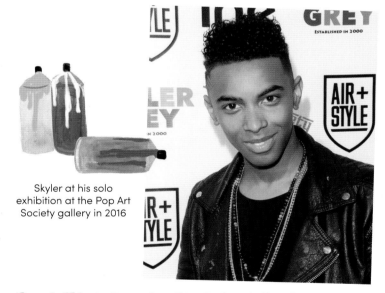

Skyler at his solo exhibition at the Pop Art Society gallery in 2016

SHAKING UP THE WORLD

These days, having left school, Skyler paints every day. While he uses traditional artist's paints or spray paints, he will also experiment with paints specially made for cars or houses to add different textures. To add sparkle, he sometimes throws ground up diamonds into the mix! Today, his paintings are bought by pop stars and fashion icons and sell for up to $60,000 each!

And Skyler's not just painting. He's working with fashion labels too, adding his touch to sneakers, jeans, and even jewelry, so if you can't afford an original, you can still own a little piece of Skyler Grey art. And beyond that? He's now planning a music career and would like to get into acting—the sky is the limit for Skyler's creativity.

SHIRLEY TEMPLE

SHIRLEY JANE TEMPLE

SHIRLEY'S CURLS

Shirley was born in 1928 in California to Gertrude and George Temple. Being the youngest of three children, and the only girl, Shirley always got a lot of attention, and every morning Gertrude fixed Shirley's hair into the ringlet curls she would become famous for.

At home, the two of them would regularly dance and sing along to music together. Even at the age of three, Shirley danced with such rhythm and style that her mother thought she could do it for a living. She signed Shirley up for dance classes and hoped that one day she would make it in the movies.

A CHANCE TO SHINE

Soon, a Hollywood producer visited the dance class, looking for children to star in some films he was making. One by one, the whole class performed—all except for two, that is. Four-year-old Shirley and her friend hid. They were too shy to dance. It was only when the producer spotted Shirley's little feet poking out from behind a piano that she came out to show what she could do. He was so impressed, he chose her to star in a series of comedy films called *Baby Burlesks*, where toddlers did silly things pretending to be adults.

Shirley doing her famous curtsy at the age of six

Nowadays, when children work on films, they are only allowed to work a few hours at a time and they must keep up with their schoolwork, but Shirley worked very long days with few breaks and no lessons. It wasn't very glamorous! As the cameras were about to roll, Gertrude would call out, "Sparkle, Shirley, sparkle!"

> **❝** TO ME [MAKING MOVIES WAS] ALWAYS A GREAT BIG GORGEOUS GAME OF LET'S-PRETEND. CHILDREN SPEND MOST OF THEIR TIME PRETENDING TO BE SOMEONE ELSE ANYHOW . . . I HAD A STUDIO FULL OF PEOPLE TO PLAY WITH ME AND ALL THE COSTUMES AND SCENERY I NEEDED. **❞**

When *Baby Burlesks* hit the movie theaters, other directors saw how good Shirley was on-screen and began choosing her for their films. In 1934, she made ten films, including *Bright Eyes* in which she sang "On the Good Ship Lollipop," a song she became well known for. Suddenly, she was getting 4,000 fan letters a week! Her face was everywhere, from cereal packets to car ads. You could buy a Shirley Temple doll or a Shirley Temple cocktail! She even got to meet the president of the United States, although she wasn't so popular with his wife, Eleanor Roosevelt. Shirley had learned how to use a slingshot for one film, *The Littlest Rebel*, and when she saw Eleanor bending over, she took aim . . . and hit!

> 66 PRESIDENT FRANKLIN D. ROOSEVELT PROCLAIMED: 'AS LONG AS OUR COUNTRY HAS SHIRLEY TEMPLE, WE WILL BE ALL RIGHT.' 99

Shirley starred in over twenty films and appeared on many colorful film posters

Shirley added her tiny hand- and footprints to the Hollywood Walk of Fame in Los Angeles

SHAKING UP THE WORLD

A few years later, Shirley was the first child ever to be awarded an Academy Juvenile Award—a "child Oscar." She went to the ceremony with her parents but by the time it was her turn to collect her award, she had fallen asleep. Later that year she added her hand- and footprints to the Hollywood Walk of Fame. By the end of 1934, Shirley had earned more money than almost everyone in Hollywood. At the age of six!

Shirley continued to make films until she was twenty-two. Then she left the movie business to work in the White House alongside the president. Her curls and sparkling smile will always be remembered and in 2005, nine years before her death, she was given a lifetime achievement award by the Screen Actors Guild.

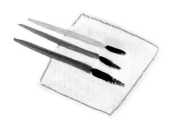

WANG YANI

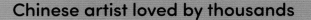

LIKE FATHER, LIKE DAUGHTER

Wang Yani was born in 1975 in Gongcheng, a small town in the south of China. Her father, Wang Shiqiang, was an artist and her mother, Tang Fongjiao, worked in a department store. One day, when Yani was almost three, she was with her father in his art studio. He was having an important meeting and Yani was bored, so she picked up a piece of charcoal and started sketching on the wall. Once she'd finished, she took a step back to admire her work, just like she'd seen her father do many times before. She was pleased, but when Shiqiang saw the charcoal on the wall, he wasn't very happy.

Another time, Yani thought she might be able to make one of her father's paintings better, so when he wasn't looking, she drew on it. This time, Shiqiang was angry. Yani burst into tears. She only wanted to paint like her father. Then, Shiqiang remembered back to when he was little. All he had ever wanted to do was paint, but his parents always told him off for making a mess. It had made him very unhappy as a child. Now that his daughter wanted to paint, he decided he would support her in any way he could.

> **❝ I THINK PAINTING IS SOMETHING VERY SIMPLE. YOU JUST PAINT WHAT YOU THINK. YOU DON'T HAVE TO FOLLOW SOMETHING. ANYONE CAN PAINT. ❞**

Shiqiang took care not to "teach" Yani— he wanted her to find her own style. Her first paintings were very simple. She drew ducks, dogs, and cats, often just as dots and squiggles, but each picture told a story that Yani would explain to her father. As she got older, her work became more complex, and one evening, when she couldn't get a painting just right, she worked on it until midnight!

THE LITTLE MONKEY PAINTER

By the age of six, Yani had painted over 4,000 pictures. She used traditional Chinese inks and brushes and painted very quickly, so her pictures felt full of energy. She drew monkeys all the time because she loved watching them when she visited the zoo. The first monkeys she sketched had the wrong number of fingers and toes, but once she learned to count, she got it right. Her painted monkeys became her friends and she'd add food for them to eat in her pictures, and butterflies and peacocks for them to play with.

People loved to watch Yani paint and would come from miles around to see her. Once, she even painted in a sports stadium in front of thousands of people! She would sometimes paint on great big sheets of Chinese rice paper spread across the floor. She would hop and skip barefoot across the paper, dabbing her brush here, swirling it there. One of her most well-known paintings, *One Hundred Monkeys*, was painted on a scroll of paper ten yards long.

Wang aged fourteen at the opening of her solo show at the Smithsonian Institution

> **WHEN YOU PICK UP A BRUSH, DON'T EVEN ASK ANYONE FOR HELP. BECAUSE THE MOST WONDERFUL THING ABOUT PAINTING IS BEING LEFT ALONE WITH YOUR OWN IMAGINATION.**

SHAKING UP THE WORLD

As more people heard of Yani's amazing paintings, she had exhibitions across the world and, at the age of fourteen, became the youngest person ever to have her own exhibition at the famous Smithsonian Institution in Washington, DC. Experts loved the freshness in her work, and the Chinese government even used four of her paintings as Chinese postage stamps.

Today, Yani still paints, but in quite a different way from when she was young. She spent years studying in Germany, where she learned new techniques. Now she is a respected artist, known across the world, combining these techniques with her traditional Chinese painting skills to create something totally new.

WANG YANI

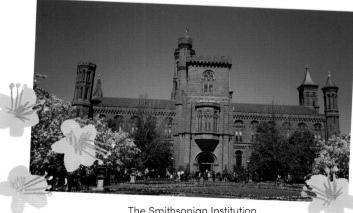

The Smithsonian Institution where Yani had her solo show

ANNE FRANK

FEAR IN GERMANY

Anne Frank was born in Frankfurt am Main in Germany in 1929. Her parents were named Otto and Edith. For the Franks, like many families in Germany at the time, life was difficult and dangerous. This was because they were Jewish, and the Nazis—a political party that many Germans supported—blamed Jewish people for everything they felt was wrong with their country. The Nazi leader, Adolf Hitler, came to power in 1933. He had a plan to get rid of all Jewish people by rounding them up and sending them to concentration camps. Millions of people were killed in these camps. Hitler's plan became known as the Final Solution, but today we know it as the Holocaust.

Otto and Edith knew that they needed to escape Germany to be safe. In 1933, they moved their family to Amsterdam in the Netherlands. Anne loved her new life and new friends in Amsterdam. Meanwhile, in Germany, Hitler set his sights on conquering Europe. In 1939, the German army marched into Poland, starting a war across Europe that became known as the Second World War. By 1940, the Nazis had invaded the Netherlands and reached Amsterdam.

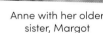

Anne with her older sister, Margot

A PLAN FORMS

The Nazis had already sent great numbers of Jewish people to their camps. The Franks knew it was only a matter of time before they would be forced to go too. With help from his friends at work, Otto hatched a plan to hide his family. In his office, there was a door hidden behind a bookcase, which led to some secret empty rooms, known as "the Secret Annex." The Frank family would hide here.

Otto Frank's office building, where he hid with Anne and the rest of the Frank family for two years

ANNELIES MARIE "ANNE" FRANK

When Anne's older sister, Margot, received a letter from the Nazis ordering her to go to a work camp, Otto knew he had to put his plan into action. In July 1942, the family went into hiding. They were joined by the Van Pels family and a dentist named Fritz Pfeffer as they began their new life of secrecy. Just before they were forced to hide, Anne had celebrated her thirteenth birthday. She was given a red-and-white-checked notebook that she used as a diary and, thanks to her writing, we know just what life was like in the secret annex.

Anne's red-and-white-checked diary, her first journal

Every day, Anne and her family had to keep as quiet as possible. Most workers in the office didn't know about the secret rooms upstairs and the slightest movement on the creaky floorboards might have given them away. They relied on friends to bring them food and books, as well as news of the war. This was dangerous. Anybody found helping Jewish people could have been sent to a work camp too.

" NO ONE HAS EVER BECOME POOR BY GIVING. "

Anne shared her innermost thoughts with her diary, pouring out her hopes, fears, and frustrations. She described how she felt guilty for being safe when she discovered her Jewish friends were being sent to camps and she wrote about her friendship with Peter Van Pels, an older boy she was in hiding with. Anne's diary was where she kept her dreams for her future and her hopes for peace, freedom, and an end to the war.

For two years Anne remained hidden until, in August 1944, the family was discovered by the Nazis. Everyone was arrested and sent to prison camps. Tragically, the only person from the secret annex to survive was Otto.

SHAKING UP THE WORLD

" I STILL BELIEVE, IN SPITE OF EVERYTHING, THAT PEOPLE ARE REALLY GOOD AT HEART. "

Once Otto returned to Amsterdam, a friend gave him Anne's diary which had been left behind. On reading the diary, Otto was so moved by his daughter's courage, talent, and imagination, he felt he must share her story with the world. Today, it is considered to be one of the most important books in history and has been published in more than sixty languages. Anne's diary shows us how cruel people can be, and her hopes for a better future act as a reminder that we must never let such things happen again.

NKOSI JOHNSON

South African activist who gave a voice to children with AIDS

A TERRIBLE ILLNESS

Nkosi Johnson's mother, Daphne, had an illness called AIDS, which is caused by a virus known as HIV. This meant that when Nkosi was born, in South Africa in 1989, he was HIV-positive. HIV, or human immunodeficiency virus, attacks parts of the body that help fight off bugs and disease. If a person with HIV can't fight infections anymore, they are said to have AIDS. Without their body's defenses, even common bugs like the cold virus can be incredibly dangerous to people living with AIDS.

When Nkosi's mother became too ill to look after Nkosi, they both went to stay at an AIDS center—a place where people living with AIDS could be cared for. Unfortunately, the center ran out of money and had to close not long after they arrived. Nkosi's mother had to find somewhere else to live, but knowing she was too ill to look after her son, she agreed to let a helper at the center, Gail Johnson, take care of Nkosi.

NKOSI JOHNSON

STOPPED FROM GOING TO SCHOOL

At the time, many babies who developed AIDS died very young, but not Nkosi. By the time he was seven, he was the longest surviving child with HIV in South Africa and Gail decided he should go to school. However, when the primary school discovered Nkosi was HIV-positive, they had other ideas.

The teachers and pupils at the school were afraid of Nkosi. People didn't yet understand how the virus spread from person to person. They thought that, as with a cold bug, they could get ill just by shaking hands or touching Nkosi. He was told he wasn't allowed to join the school.

❝ DON'T BE AFRAID OF US, WE ARE ALL THE SAME. YOU CAN'T GET AIDS IF YOU TOUCH, HUG, KISS, HOLD HANDS WITH SOMEONE WHO IS INFECTED. ❞

Gail was very angry. She wanted people to know the truth about AIDS, so she started telling Nkosi's story to journalists. They interviewed Nkosi and he talked about how you could only catch the virus from his infected blood or saliva. He wanted people to know that you couldn't catch AIDS from playing together and he wasn't a danger to other children.

Eventually, the school accepted him. Not only that, they started classes for teachers and pupils that taught them the facts about AIDS. Soon, the South African government made it illegal to stop children going to school just because they had AIDS.

> **CARE FOR US AND ACCEPT US—WE ARE ALL HUMAN BEINGS. WE ARE NORMAL. WE HAVE HANDS. WE HAVE FEET. WE CAN WALK, WE CAN TALK, WE HAVE NEEDS JUST LIKE EVERYONE ELSE—DON'T BE AFRAID OF US—WE ARE ALL THE SAME!**

It was a great victory, but it wasn't enough. Nkosi wanted to raise enough money to build a home where people with AIDS could come for help, just like his mother had done when he was a baby. Finally, in 1999, after years of campaigning, Nkosi and Gail had raised enough money to open Nkosi's Haven, a center to provide support and shelter to mothers and children with AIDS.

Nkosi with his adopted mother, Gail

SHAKING UP THE WORLD

A year later, Nkosi was asked to speak at a big international conference about HIV. Although he was getting more and more ill, he knew it was important to keep campaigning. He asked for South Africans to care for and accept people living with AIDS, then demanded that the South African government do more to help them. When he finished his speech, the audience got to their feet and cheered him. His words were reported around the world and put pressure on the South African president to do something to help.

Soon after this speech Nkosi became very unwell and died peacefully in his sleep. He was only twelve years old. Thousands of people came to his funeral and he became a symbol of the injustice and cruelty of living with HIV in South Africa. After his death, in 2005 he was awarded the first International Children's Peace Prize.

> **DO ALL YOU CAN WITH WHAT YOU HAVE IN THE TIME YOU HAVE IN THE PLACE YOU ARE.**

GULWALI PASSARLAY

Afghan refugee who survived against the odds

ESCAPE FROM AFGHANISTAN

Gulwali Passarlay was born in Afghanistan in 1994, the son of a doctor and a midwife. When he was just seven years old, the US invaded his country and Gulwali's town became a war zone. His family often had to run to escape bombs and rockets. One day, his father was killed in an attack on their home. His mother knew if twelve-year-old Gulwali and his brother Hazrat stayed in Afghanistan, they would be in great danger.

She decided to do something drastic to save her sons. She paid $8,000 to people traffickers, who promised they would smuggle the two boys out of the country to start a new, safer life in Europe. But neither brother realized how terrifying this journey would be.

HEADING FOR EUROPE

Almost immediately, the smugglers separated the two boys. Gulwali traveled by night, sleeping on the floors of cold trucks and vans. His route to Europe took him across the Mediterranean Sea and here the smugglers forced 120 refugees onto a boat big enough for just 20. They spent over two days on the water without food or drink and by the time they were rescued, their boat was sinking. Gulwali only just made it to Europe alive.

> 66 FORGET BEING TREATED LIKE A CHILD, I WASN'T EVEN TREATED LIKE A HUMAN. 99

Next came a real-life game of chutes and ladders his smugglers took him on a roundabout ride arou Europe. Without a passport, if he was stopped by the police, he could be thrown in jail or sent back t Afghanistan, so he crossed borders hidden in tract trailers, desperately looking for somewhere to call home. Eventually, he made it to France.

Gulwali knew his brother Hazrat had wanted to get to Britain, so Gulwali decided to head there too. Hundreds of trucks traveled across the English Channel each day, so if he could hide in one, he might manage to avoid the police. He tried over one hundred times, but each time he was spotted and thrown off the truck. Finally, in 2007, one year after leaving Afghanistan, and smuggled in a truck full of bananas, Gulwali arrived in Britain.

Almost immediately, he was arrested by British border police, who took him to an immigration center for questioning. They believed he was sixteen, not thirteen. This was important, because while a thirteen-year-old would be allowed to stay in Britain, go to school, and be cared for by a foster family, a sixteen-year-old would be treated like an adult and sent home.

Eventually, he convinced the authorities that he was only a child and was given permission to stay. At last, he was safe.

GULWALI PASSARLAY

Gulwali, at age ten, with his younger brother, Nasir, at home in Afghanistan (above) and Gulwali today (right)

SHAKING UP THE WORLD

Gulwali started school and was placed in a home with wonderful foster parents, who made him feel secure and loved. Even better, he tracked down his brother who, incredibly, had made it safely to the UK too.

But Gulwali remembered how tough both his journey and arrival in Britain had been and wanted to help others in similar situations. He became a school ambassador, helping refugees who were often scared, lonely, and confused, to feel safe when they arrived.

Gulwali went on to study politics in college and later set up an organization to help refugees arriving in Britain. Today, he campaigns for refugees around the world because he hopes that one day, no children will ever have to experience the hardship he went through just to find a safe place to call home.

The beautiful countryside of Gulwali's home in Afghanistan

"IF THINGS HAD BEEN EASY FOR ME, I WOULDN'T BE HERE NOW. EVERY DAY IS AN OPPORTUNITY AND I DON'T WANT TO WASTE IT."

MARLEY DIAS

BORN TO READ

Marley Dias was born in 2005 in Philadelphia, Pennsylvania, and has always loved stories. As soon as she learned to read, her nose was always in a book.

Once Marley started middle school, her teachers gave her books, but they weren't as enjoyable as the ones she read at home. The heroes in these stories all seemed to be white boys. Marley wanted to see herself in the stories instead! She wanted to read books about girls of color—girls like her! Marley knew these books were out there—she had plenty at home and when her mom and dad took her to the big bookstore in town, she'd seen lots more—but the teachers never seemed to hand these books out.

MARLEY DIAS

> **66** ANYONE CAN CHANGE THE WORLD HOWEVER THEY WANT FOR THE BETTER. **99**

Marley realized there were other girls, perhaps not lucky enough to be taken to bookstores, or unable to afford books, who should have the chance to read the same kind of stories as her. She discussed the problem with her mom, who asked what Marley was going to do about it. If there's one thing Marley loves almost as much as books, it's a challenge!

CAMPAIGNING AND COLLECTING

So, along with a couple of friends, Marley started a campaign to collect 1,000 books in which a black girl or girl of color is the main character in the story—not the friend of the hero, not someone the hero meets on the way, but the person right in the center of the picture. The plan was to donate these books to schools and libraries in Jamaica, where her mom had been born. She called the campaign 1000BlackGirlBooks and started using social media to get her message out.

Soon readers and authors across the country started sending Marley books. She appeared in magazines and newspapers and even on one of the biggest talk shows on television, which meant many more people around the world got to find out what she was doing. She quickly collected the 1,000 books. In fact, she soon had over 11,000, and they're still coming in today.

The books have been sent to Jamaica, but as well as providing great reading material for the schoolgirls there, Marley's campaign revealed how most children's books published are about white boys and girls. Children everywhere should be able to read stories about people just like them and Marley's campaign has made people take notice.

> 66 MY PASSION FOR BOOKS HAS CHANGED MY LIFE. 99

Marley got to write her own book, *Marley Dias Gets It Done: And So Can You!*, which came out in January 2018

SHAKING UP THE WORLD

Stories have always taken Marley on journeys, but her book campaign has taken her on an amazing real-life adventure. Through 1000BlackGirlBooks, she's met two of the most important women in American politics, Michelle Obama and Hillary Clinton, won *Smithsonian Magazine*'s American Ingenuity Youth Award, and even made the list of the thirty most influential people in America under the age of thirty—at just twelve years old.

Marley appearing in an article for the *Smithsonian Magazine* (left) and speaking at The New York Women's Foundation in 2017 (right)

> 66 BLACK GIRL STORIES AREN'T JUST FOR BLACK GIRLS: THEY'RE FOR EVERYBODY. 99

Now Marley wants other young people to stand up and make a difference too. And she's even added a very special book to the 1000BlackGirlBooks list—her own! *Marley Dias Gets It Done: And So Can You!* shares her passion for making our world a better place and helps readers make their dreams come true.

MALALA YOUSAFZAI

DESPERATE TO LEARN

Malala Yousafzai was born in 1997 in a place called the Swat Valley in Pakistan. Many girls in Pakistan aren't sent to school, but Malala's parents believed she should be educated just like her brothers. Malala's father, Ziauddin, was a teacher and soon Malala was enjoying her studies at his school, working hard, and winning prizes. That was until the Taliban arrived.

The Taliban—a group of extreme politicians and religious preachers—had very strict views on how people should live their lives. They believed listening to music or watching television was wrong. They expected women and girls to stay at home to look after the men in the family, instead of going to school or work, and they punished people who disobeyed their rules.

The Taliban wanted to control the Swat Valley and put a stop to girls going to school. Bravely, Malala's father kept his school open and, even though she was scared, Malala continued to go to lessons. To keep herself safe from the Taliban, she stopped wearing her school uniform and even hid her school books.

> **❝ HOW DARE THE TALIBAN TAKE MY EDUCATION AWAY. ❞**

The BBC, a television company in the UK, was looking for a young person to write a diary for their website about what it was like to live under the Taliban's rule. They knew Malala's father had spoken out against the Taliban, so they contacted him to see if he knew of anyone. He suggested it to Malala. She agreed, but only if she could use a made-up name to hide her identity. So, in 2009, aged eleven, Malala began her blog to reveal how unfair life was for girls and women in the Swat Valley.

54

TARGETED BY THE TALIBAN

Meanwhile, the Pakistani army was fighting to drive the Taliban away. Life became very dangerous and Malala's family fled. Malala wrote about this in her diary and soon people around the world began to take notice. Journalists quickly discovered who the secret writer was. In her own way, Malala was fighting the Taliban, using words instead of guns.

Eventually the fighting stopped and Malala's family returned home. Her father reopened his school and Malala started lessons again. She received Pakistan's first National Youth Peace Prize and was nominated for the International Children's Peace Prize. But the Taliban hadn't disappeared and they were angry at Malala for speaking out against them.

One afternoon in October 2012, Malala was sitting with her friends on the school bus when a young boy got on. He approached Malala, raised a gun, and fired it at her three times. Believing she was dead, the boy ran away.

But amazingly, Malala had survived. She was rushed to the hospital, where doctors removed a bullet from her brain. She was then flown to England, where the bones in her skull were rebuilt and she had an electronic device fitted to help her damaged hearing. After three months, she was well enough to leave the hospital.

MALALA YOUSAFZAI

Malala and her father, Ziauddin, at the United Nations Headquarters in New York City (above) and Malala's book, *I Am Malala* (left)

SHAKING UP THE WORLD

The Taliban's plan was to silence Malala, but it didn't work. After her incredible recovery, her story was heard around the world. She wrote a bestselling book about her life that was made into an award-winning film. World leaders, including the president of the United States, wanted to meet her. She was even invited to talk at the United Nations, a global organization that meets to discuss world matters and concerns.

❝ I DON'T WANT TO BE THOUGHT OF AS THE 'GIRL WHO WAS SHOT BY THE TALIBAN' BUT THE 'GIRL WHO FOUGHT FOR EDUCATION.' THIS IS THE CAUSE TO WHICH I WANT TO DEVOTE MY LIFE. ❞

Today, Malala continues to campaign for free education for all children wherever they are. Her bravery and persistence in standing up to the wrongs she experienced has earned her many awards. At the age of seventeen, she became the youngest person ever to win the Nobel Peace Prize, the highest award for promoting peace in the world, which shows how one brave schoolgirl really can make a world of difference.

MOMČILO GAVRIĆ

A FAMILY GONE

Momčilo Gavrić was born in 1906 and lived in a small village in Serbia with his mother, father, and ten brothers and sisters. In August 1914, war broke out. Serbia was being attacked by its neighbor, the Austro-Hungarian Empire, and soon other countries joined in the fighting. Today, we know it as the First World War.

One day, eight-year-old Momčilo was visiting his uncle's house in Trbušnica, a nearby village. His family didn't realize the danger they were in, but when Momčilo returned, he discovered enemy soldiers had killed his parents and burned down his home. If any of his brothers and sisters were still alive, they had fled. Momčilo didn't know what to do. He was now an orphan, alone and scared.

Momčilo with another soldier in his specially made army uniform

THE YOUNGEST RECRUIT

Then, as he was wandering through the countryside, Momčilo came across a group of Serbian soldiers. When they discovered what had happened to the young boy, the soldiers felt sorry for him. But Momčilo didn't want their pity. He was angry and he wanted revenge.

Momčilo led his new friends to where the remains of his house lay smoldering. From here, they traced the path of the enemy soldiers until they could see their camp in the distance. Then the Serbian troops started firing at the Austro-Hungarians. Momčilo even helped, desperate to prevent the soldiers from taking away another boy's family.

Without a home, Momčilo had nowhere to go and no one to look after him. The Serbian troops became his family. One soldier in particular, Miloš Mišović, took special care of him. He taught Momčilo how to handle a gun and how to keep himself safe from the enemy.

Just days later, Momčilo's soldier friends were ordered into battle in the Cer Mountains in Serbia. More enemy troops were attacking. For over a week, Momčilo helped by running messages between the generals and the front line. He was very lucky to survive. Momčilo's army unit was so impressed with the way he had performed, they had a uniform made especially for him and awarded him the rank of corporal. As he saluted his comrades, he was proud to be the newest, and youngest ever, recruit in the Serbian Army.

Serbian soldiers in battle during the First World War

SHAKING UP THE WORLD

Momčilo had made good friends in the army, but life was hard. By 1915, the Serbians were losing the war and they were forced to move back over a great mountain range into Greece, where they would be safe. Momčilo marched and marched across freezing slopes with barely enough food to survive. It was exhausting, and Momčilo's friend Miloš collapsed in the snow. Momčilo tried to haul him to his feet, but he was too heavy. Miloš told Momčilo to keep marching and save himself, but Momčilo refused.

Instead, he lay down next to his friend and prepared for the two of them to die. Miloš couldn't allow the young soldier to lose his life there, so, incredibly, he found the strength to keep walking. Momčilo had saved Miloš's life and, eventually, the soldiers reached the safety of Greece.

Finally, in 1918, peace was declared. After the war, Momčilo was sent to school in England before returning to Serbia, where he was able to track down three of his brothers who had survived the attack on their home all those years ago. Many people showed great bravery during the war, but there were few eight-year-olds as brave as Momčilo. His name may not be well known across the world, but he is often remembered in his own country as the youngest soldier in the First World War, who was prepared to lay down his life for a friend.

MOMČILO GAVRIĆ

Momčilo was sent to school in England after the war, before going back home to Serbia

MICHAELA MYCROFT

FLOWERPOTS AND WHEELCHAIRS

Michaela, or Chaeli, Mycroft was born in 1994 in Cape Town, South Africa. When she was eleven months old, doctors realized she had a condition called cerebral palsy. Chaeli's brain wasn't able to send messages to the rest of her body like most people's do, so moving, walking, and even talking was difficult.

Chaeli got used to being in a wheelchair, but by the time she was nine she was tired of relying on other people to push her around. Motorized wheelchairs were very expensive, so Chaeli and her sister and friends decided to raise the money. They sold homemade greeting cards and plants in hand-painted flowerpots and quickly raised the $1,500 needed for the wheelchair.

> ❝ YOU HAVE TO HELP A PERSON TO SEE THEIR OWN GREATNESS. ❞

Chaeli was thrilled with her new wheelchair: she loved the independence it gave her and wanted other disabled children to have that same feeling. But she knew that in some areas of South Africa many disabled children were ignored or forgotten. Some children didn't go to school, and many couldn't even read or write. Chaeli understood why. Schools would need to build ramps and special toilets for people who used wheelchairs, and teachers might need extra training to teach students with disabilities—all of this costs money.

CAMPAIGNING FOR ALL

Chaeli wanted to help, so she and her friends carried on raising money for other disabled children. However, Chaeli wanted to do something even more important: she wanted to change the way people thought about disabled people. As she was growing up, she'd talked openly about her disability with her family. It wasn't something to be embarrassed about or ashamed of, it was just how life was. But Chaeli realized some people felt awkward or uncomfortable discussing disability with her. She thought this was silly. Surely the more disability was talked about, the more people would understand the challenges Chaeli and others faced.

She believed that if children mixed more, they would soon discover that they all had similar hopes, dreams, and ambitions. Eventually, her charity, the Chaeli Campaign, raised enough money to open an inclusive preschool that could teach children of all abilities together. By the time Chaeli was seventeen, there were twenty-two people working for her charity across South Africa. They help disabled children with practical things like wheelchairs, but they also campaign for disabled children to be included in society more.

MICHAELA "CHAELI" MYCROFT

" IT'S EMPOWERING TO HAVE A WHEELCHAIR. IT'S NOT A NEGATIVE THING. "

Chaeli at her home in Cape Town, South Africa (top) and visiting the Chaeli Campaign, which supports disabled children in South Africa (bottom)

Chaeli was called a "disability activist" but she prefers the name "ability activist," because it focuses on all the things she can do, not what she can't. If people see her doing extraordinary things, then they might start to see disabled people as no better or worse than themselves, just different.

" A LOT OF PEOPLE SEE ME AS A DISABILITY ACTIVIST. I DON'T. I FOCUS ON THE ABILITY. "

SHAKING UP THE WORLD

Chaeli has collected many awards, including the Peace Summit Medal, the World of Children Award, and the International Children's Peace Prize. Today, she campaigns for disabled people across South Africa, raising money and awareness by taking on some incredible challenges.

In 2015, Chaeli became the first woman without working arms and legs to reach the top of Mount Kilimanjaro, the highest mountain in Africa, proving that nothing can stop you if you're determined to succeed.

Chaeli was helped up Mount Kilimanjaro, Africa's highest mountain, by her amazing team, the Chaeli Kili Climbers

CALVIN GRAHAM

US sailor who won medals for his bravery in the Second World War

CALVIN LEON GRAHAM

U.S. NAVY

WANTING TO FIGHT

Calvin Graham was born in 1930 in Canton, Texas. His father died when he was little and his mother remarried, but Calvin's stepfather did not treat Calvin well, so, at the age of eleven, he moved out and found a job delivering letters and selling newspapers.

Every day, Calvin read the headlines of his newspapers and he soon learned of the war going on in Europe. In 1941, America joined the war, and Calvin's cousins joined the US Army to fight. Calvin wanted to help too.

TRIBUNE

INVASION

The DAILY
WAR DECLARED IN EUROPE

He decided to join the US Navy, a group of soldiers who fight for their country at sea. The trouble was, you had to be seventeen, so he would have to pretend to be much older than he was. He started shaving in the hope that hair would grow on his chin, but when it didn't, he practiced speaking in a deep voice instead.

IN THE NAVY

When he went to sign up, Calvin wore his older brother's clothes, thinking they would make him look older, but when the navy doctor examined inside his mouth, he knew straightaway that Calvin was underage. He still had some of his baby teeth! Calvin insisted he was seventeen, and even though the medic knew he must have been younger, eventually, he let Calvin through.

Calvin told his mother he was going to visit relatives, when actually he was off to a navy training camp. The instructors there suspected he was underage too, so they pushed him to train harder, run farther, and carry a heavier backpack than anyone else to force him to drop out. Instead, it made Calvin want to succeed even more. He became the youngest person to serve for the US in the Second World War, at the age of twelve years, four months, and twelve days.

❝IT WAS A LONG NIGHT. IT AGED ME.❞

Calvin served on the warship USS *South Dakota* and sailed to the South Pacific to fight enemy ships. Just after his thirteenth birthday, he took part in one of the most important sea battles of the Second World War—the Battle of Guadalcanal.

SHAKING UP THE WORLD

Calvin was blown down three flights of stairs when the *South Dakota* was hit by enemy shells. He broke his jaw, lost two teeth, and was badly burned, but he was still alive. Many weren't so lucky. Despite his injuries, Calvin spent a long night helping other sailors to safety.

❝I DIDN'T DO ANY COMPLAINING BECAUSE HALF THE SHIP WAS DEAD. IT WAS A WHILE BEFORE THEY WORKED ON MY MOUTH.❞

After Guadalcanal, Calvin returned home and was awarded Purple Heart and Bronze Star medals for his bravery. When his mother saw him in his smart uniform, she was furious. He had gone to war without telling her! She didn't want her thirteen-year-old son going back to fight, so she told the navy he had been lying about his age.

The Battle of Guadalcanal went on for six months and two days (top) and Bronze Star and Purple Heart medals like the ones Calvin received (bottom)

Even though Calvin was put in prison for three months and stripped of his medals, he was determined to serve in the armed forces again. Eventually, when he was old enough, he joined the US Marines, but it wasn't long before he damaged his back in an accident and had to leave.

Calvin aged twelve in his Navy uniform

Calvin never served in the armed forces again, but he was most upset about having his medals taken away. It was true that he had been underage, but hadn't he still shown great bravery? Very few knew about his story until he was an old man, when a film was made about his life. When people heard of the boy who had been too young to be a hero, a campaign was started to get his medals returned and, in 1994, two years after his death, they were returned to his family.

MOHAMAD AL JOUNDE

Syrian refugee who built a school to call his own

TOUGH TIMES

Mohamad Al Jounde was born in Syria in 2001. His mother was a math teacher and his father an artist. He had a close family, good friends, and a nice house to call home. But, sadly, things were about to change.

President al-Assad had ruled Syria since before Mohamad was born, but many Syrians, including Mohamad's mother, didn't think he was a good, or fair, leader. By 2011, many Syrians wanted a new ruler, but President al-Assad wasn't going to go without a fight. Soon, there was war across the country, as people tried to force Assad and his followers from power.

MOHAMAD AL JOUNDE

Mohamad's mother got into trouble because she had spoken out against Assad. The army threatened to kill her unless she left the country. So, along with thousands of others, Mohamad and his family fled from Syria to Beirut, the capital city of their neighboring country, Lebanon. Now Mohamad was a refugee.

BUILDING A SCHOOL

In Lebanon, Mohamad and his family were safe from the fighting, but they had lost their home, their community, their friends, and their belongings. As a refugee, Mohamad wasn't allowed to go to a Lebanese school and he really missed his lessons. School had given him a place to meet friends and he knew how important education was for his future. So, he had an idea. He would start his own school and create a new community for him and other Syrian refugees.

Mohamad thought about what subjects to teach, how many pupils and teachers he would need, and how much it would all cost. He then asked a charity that supported refugees for money to help set up his project. He knew they would never agree to a twelve-year-old's idea, so he persuaded his mother to add her name so that it looked like a grown-up's proposal. And not just any grown-up—Mohamad's mom was a teacher!

> **EVERY CHILD HAS THE RIGHT TO LEARN AND THE RIGHT TO GO TO SCHOOL.**

To his amazement, the charity thought his plan was fantastic and agreed to help. In 2014, Mohamad's school for Syrian refugees opened. He called it Gharsah School—the Arabic word for "sprout"—because this was a place for ideas, friendship, and hope to sprout and grow.

The school started off in a small tent but, over time, the number of pupils doubled, and the Gharsah School got its own building. Instead of being a pupil as he had been in Syria, Mohamad ended up teaching—math, English, and his real love, photography. He understood that many refugee children had experienced dreadful things that they often struggled to talk about, but he knew that sharing their stories could make them feel better. He discovered that some children found it easier to express themselves through photographs, like he did, so he encouraged his pupils to use a camera to tell their stories.

Mohamad making his acceptance speech for the International Children's Peace Prize

> **I FELT HAPPY TO BE NOT JUST A TEACHER, BUT A FRIEND, AND WE BECAME A FAMILY— WE ARE STRONGER TOGETHER.**

SHAKING UP THE WORLD

The war in Syria has lasted over seven years and more than 4.5 million people like Mohamad have fled the country. Mohamad is now continuing his education in Sweden, but his school in Beirut is still open—educating children, and, importantly, helping them to recover from the trauma they have lived through. Mohamad knows that Syria's future depends on the education of its children and for his extraordinary work in setting up the Gharsah School, Malala Yousafzai presented him with the International Children's Peace Prize in 2017.

Mohamad being awarded the prize by Malala Yousafzai in 2017

HANNAH TAYLOR

ON THE STREET

Hannah Taylor was born in Winnipeg, Canada, in 1996. One day, when she was about five, Hannah and her mother were driving home together after a day out. It was bitterly cold outside, but they were cozy and warm in the car.

As they drove through the town, Hannah spotted a man on the sidewalk, looking very scruffy. He was rummaging around in a trash can searching for food. Hannah was confused. Why did the man look so dirty? And why was he eating food from the trash? Hannah's mother explained that he was homeless, and didn't have anywhere to live. Each night, he slept on the streets and, with no money, he found food wherever he could.

" CHANGE USUALLY COMES FROM MORE UNDERSTANDING. "

A cold winter's day in Winnipeg, Canada, where people ice-skate on the frozen Red River

HANNAH TAYLOR

For months afterward, Hannah couldn't forget the homeless man she'd seen. At teatime, she'd wonder what he was eating. At bedtime, she'd imagine where he might be sleeping. She became so concerned about him that, one night, her mother said the best way to stop worrying was to do something about it.

" IF YOU DEEPLY BELIEVE IN SOMETHING . . . YOU CAN MAKE CHANGE IN THE WORLD FOR BETTER. "

So, that's exactly what Hannah did. She went to visit a homeless shelter—a place where homeless people can get food and hot drinks—to see how she could help. When she was shown around, she burst into tears of relief. Now she had found a way she could help the homeless.

Hannah aged ten speaking about her Ladybug Foundation

LUCKY LADYBUGS

Hannah set about raising money for the shelter. She found some old jars and painted them red with black dots and wings to turn them into ladybug collecting jars. Many people think of ladybugs, or ladybirds, as lucky, so Hannah hoped these brightly colored jars would help homeless people who were down on their luck. She handed them out to schools and businesses to collect people's spare change.

> **" SOMEBODY HAS TO MAKE A DIFFERENCE IN PEOPLE'S LIVES. SOMEBODY NEEDS TO BE A LEADER. "**

Alongside the jars, she organized Big Boss Lunches, where she'd sit down with the leaders of local businesses with sandwiches and juice. They would discuss how hard life was for homeless people and Hannah would persuade them to help her cause. Sometimes she would bring along pictures she had painted to sell and once someone paid $10,000 for her artwork! Eventually, Hannah was raising so much money she set up an official charity, the Ladybug Foundation, to help homeless shelters and food banks across Canada.

But Hannah did more than that. She also volunteered in the shelters she was raising money for. Hannah treated the homeless people in the shelters with kindness and compassion. She understood that they needed someone to care for them and love them. Once, as she gave a homeless man a hug, he burst into tears. It had been so long since anyone had hugged him, he had forgotten what it felt like!

Hannah started a "Red Scarf Day" in her city to draw attention to the thousands of homeless people

SHAKING UP THE WORLD

Since Hannah started her Ladybug Foundation, in 2004, it has raised over $4 million for homeless people. The foundation also runs an education program called makeChange, which gives children the skills needed to change things they care passionately about. So far, it's been taught in over 11,000 classrooms.

For this, Hannah has won award after award, and was even included on a 100 Most Powerful Women list when she was only eleven years old! Today, Hannah is concentrating on her studies, hoping one day to become a lawyer so that in the future her compassion can help even more people.

PELÉ

A STRIKER IS BORN

Pelé was born in the city of Três Corações, in the southeast of Brazil in 1940. His parents named him Edson Arantes do Nascimento: the nickname, Pelé, came later.

Pelé's father, João Ramos, was a professional soccer player known as Dondinho, but he wasn't very successful. It meant the family didn't have very much money. Pelé often went without shoes, and sometimes meals were just a slice of bread and a banana.

Nevertheless, Pelé was happy. He used to swim in the nearby river, make dens in the woods, and, of course, play soccer. Unfortunately, his family couldn't afford to buy a ball, so Pelé and his friends made do with a sock stuffed with paper or rags.

Pelé became the youngest ever winner of a World Cup aged just seventeen

He got the name Pelé as a little boy. It is thought to have come from when he cheered on his father's soccer team—the goalkeeper's name was Bilé but Pelé would pronounce it wrong, shouting, "Pelé! Pelé! Pelé!" From then on, the name stuck.

❝ THERE'S ALWAYS SOMEONE OUT THERE GETTING BETTER THAN YOU BY TRAINING HARDER THAN YOU. ❞

BUILDING A TEAM

Pelé and his friends wanted to become a real soccer team and play in a league, but with no ball, no gear, and no cleats, no one would let them play. They needed to earn money fast, so the boys came up with moneymaking schemes.

The 1950 World Cup was approaching. They thought they could sell completed World Cup sticker books to raise enough money—but they couldn't afford enough stickers to complete a book. They trawled the streets looking for scrap metal they could sell, but discovered there was little spare scrap to be found. Pelé finally found a way to make money—selling peanuts to customers at the local movie theater.

Eventually, the team earned enough to buy themselves shorts and jerseys. A local businessman agreed to buy their cleats. Now that Pelé was part of a real team, he could begin to get noticed. All the while, Pelé practiced and practiced his soccer skills. His father taught him how to pass and shoot with both feet, how to use a change of speed, a shoulder feint or dummy to send a defender the wrong way, and how to head the ball. Pelé was a natural.

When Pelé was just thirteen, a talent scout from one of the biggest clubs in Brazil, Santos, heard about his raw natural talent and came to see him play. After watching Pelé for just a few minutes, the scout stopped the game and wouldn't leave until the boy had signed for his club. Pelé moved to Santos when he was fifteen and became the youngest player ever to play first-class soccer, scoring a goal in his first game!

> **" SUCCESS ISN'T DETERMINED BY HOW MANY TIMES YOU WIN, BUT BY HOW YOU PLAY THE WEEK AFTER YOU LOSE. "**

EDSON ARANTES DO NASCIMENTO

Pelé playing against Belgium in 1968, where he performed his famous overhead kick

SHAKING UP THE WORLD

In 1957, Pelé finished his first season at Santos as top scorer. The crowds loved him. He was fast, strong, good with both feet, creative, and smart and it was no surprise when he made the national team at just sixteen. A year later, he went on to play in the 1958 World Cup in Sweden, making it all the way to the final against the hosts. Brazil won 5—2, with Pelé scoring two goals. He became a Brazilian national hero and is still the youngest person ever to win a World Cup.

Today, Pelé is admired by sports fans around the world. During his glittering career, he scored over 1,200 goals, and he's still the only player to have won the World Cup three times. His sense of fair play saw him become minister for sport for Brazil and he was voted Athlete of the Century by the International Olympic Committee. Many believe Pelé is, quite simply, the greatest soccer player ever.

BRAZIL, 1958.

Pelé (front row, third from the left) and the winning Brazilian soccer team at the 1958 World Cup in Sweden

> **" SUCCESS IS NO ACCIDENT. IT IS HARD WORK, PERSEVERANCE, LEARNING, STUDYING, SACRIFICE, AND MOST OF ALL, LOVE OF WHAT YOU ARE DOING OR LEARNING TO DO. "**

LAURA DEKKER

BORN TO SAIL

Laura Dekker was born in New Zealand in 1995. Her parents, Dick and Babs, were sailing around the world together and had stopped in New Zealand to live and work for a while before setting sail again. By the time they made it back home to the Netherlands, Laura was five years old.

Having spent so much of her early life on the water, it's no surprise Laura loved to sail. She got her first boat at the age of six, a little tub of a boat she called *Guppy*, and before long she was exploring the coastline of the Netherlands. Soon she had hatched a plan to do just what her parents had done . . . sail around the world. The only difference was Laura was still a child and she wanted to sail alone.

A CROSS-CHANNEL CHALLENGE

Dick knew how tough a round-the-world trip would be, so he set Laura a challenge to make sure she knew what she was up against. She was to sail to England across the English Channel. Although the distance is only 112 miles, the Channel is one of the busiest and most difficult stretches of water in the world to sail.

So, one day in May 2009, thirteen-year-old Laura set sail. She didn't tell her father where she was going but surprised him some days later by sending an e-mail from England. Dick was impressed that she'd managed the crossing, but the British authorities weren't. They were angry that a young girl had been allowed to sail the dangerous Channel alone. They demanded Dick came to pick Laura up and sail her boat back to the Netherlands himself. Dick did fly to England, but he simply put Laura back on her boat, and waved goodbye as she set sail across the Channel . . . alone!

Now fourteen, Laura felt she was ready to sail around the world. However, this time it was the Dutch authorities that weren't happy. They insisted she was too young and needed to wait a year before she could begin. Finally, on August 21, 2010, she set sail from Gibraltar, just off the Spanish coast.

Laura on board *Guppy* during filming for *Maidentrip*, a documentary about her voyage filmed in 2013

66 I HAVE CONSCIOUSLY FACED THE FEAR OF THE UNKNOWN, CONFRONTED MYSELF, AND CONQUERED ANXIETIES AND LONELINESS. I'VE BECOME STRONGER MENTALLY AND FEEL ON TOP OF THE WORLD. **99**

LAURA DEKKER

Laura was sailing a special forty-foot yacht she also named *Guppy*. The sailing was tough—tougher than anything she'd ever experienced. At times, *Guppy* was tossed around as if on a roller coaster, pounded by twenty-foot waves. Laura had to clip herself to the boat in case she was swept overboard, and water would pour through the deck, soaking her bed and clothes.
A flying fish once hit her in the face and for some of the voyage she was worried about pirates. To top it all, she even had to keep up with her schoolwork!

But despite the dangers, Laura loved the adventure and was blissfully happy being out on the high seas alone. Dolphins and whales swam alongside her, penguins and seals watched her sail by, and seeing the miles of blue sea ahead of her made her heart sing.

> **THERE WERE MOMENTS WHERE I WAS LIKE, 'WHAT THE HELL AM I DOING OUT HERE?' BUT I NEVER WANTED TO STOP.**

SHAKING UP THE WORLD

Finally, one year and five months after she'd left Gibraltar, Laura arrived at the Caribbean port of Saint Maarten. She was just sixteen years and 123 days old and is still the youngest person ever to sail solo around the world. She had shown real determination and extraordinary bravery to achieve her life's ambition at such a young age but, amazingly, she wasn't finished yet. Almost as soon as Laura had completed her epic journey, she set sail again, this time for New Zealand where she'd been born. Just like her parents, years earlier, Laura has made the country her home. Who knows what challenges await her there?

ELLIE SIMMONDS

British Paralympic swimming champion

A SPECIAL SWIMMER

Ellie Simmonds was born in 1994 in Walsall, near Birmingham, England, the youngest of five children. Even from a young age, Ellie was always busy. She spent hours in the swimming pool in her back garden, she had dance classes, went to Brownies, and rode ponies. She never stopped.

Ellie was born with a condition called achondroplasia, also known as dwarfism, which affected how some of her bones grew. It meant her arms and legs would always be quite short, but it didn't stop Ellie living a very active life: she threw herself into everything she tried.

> **66** GIVE EVERYTHING YOU'VE GOT AND ALWAYS TRY YOUR BEST AT EVERYTHING. **99**

Swimming was Ellie's favorite activity and when she was just seven, she entered her first big swimming competition. Sadly, she didn't win, but one of the organizers told Ellie that for someone with achondroplasia she was very, very fast. It made Ellie determined to train even harder, and when she was ten, she entered her first swimming meet for disabled sportsmen and women.

Ellie training at her local swimming pool

> **66** BELIEVE IN YOURSELF AND FOLLOW YOUR DREAM. DOING SO NEEDS HARD WORK AND DEDICATION, BUT IT'S DEFINITELY WORTH IT. **99**

On the day of the competition, Ellie was shocked to discover who she was swimming against: the Welsh swimmer Nyree Lewis. Just months earlier, Ellie had watched Nyree win a gold medal at the Athens Paralympics, the Olympic Games for competitors with impairments. Now Ellie was racing against her!

Ellie didn't beat Nyree, but she realized she was good enough to compete with the best. Soon after, she represented Great Britain at the 2006 Swimming World Championship in Durban, South Africa. She was the youngest on the British team by far and, although she didn't win, she swam faster than she'd ever swum before.

DREAM TO WIN

Ellie had a natural talent but, to be the best, she needed specialist coaching. Unfortunately, the nearest coach lived over 150 miles away, in Swansea, Wales. To reach the top, Ellie would have to move home, change schools, and say goodbye to her friends. It was a difficult decision, but she took the plunge. Training was tough. She swam before and after school, and Saturday mornings too—eighteen hours a week in all!

A gold medal from the London 2012 Paralympic Games

But the hard work all seemed to pay off when, in 2008, at the age of thirteen, she found herself in Beijing, China, as the youngest member of the British Paralympic Team. It was a close finish in the 100-meter freestyle . . . but Ellie won! When her name came up on the winner's board, she burst into tears. She couldn't believe she had just won a gold medal at the Paralympics! And her success didn't end there, as she went on to win another gold in the 400-meter freestyle. When she got back to the UK, Ellie was given a special award by the queen called an MBE, making her the youngest person ever to receive one.

ELEANOR MAY "ELLIE" SIMMONDS

SHAKING UP THE WORLD

Four years later, Ellie competed in the 2012 London Paralympics. At eighteen, she was no longer a newcomer and she felt the pressure in front of a home crowd. But Ellie didn't disappoint, and she finished with an incredible haul of medals— two gold, one silver, and one bronze—as well as clocking up world record times. At the Rio Paralympics in 2016, she went on to beat records again and win her fifth gold medal.

❝ I CAN DO EVERYTHING EVERYONE ELSE CAN DO. IF I WASN'T SMALL, I WOULDN'T HAVE GONE TO THE PARALYMPICS. ❞

Today, Ellie supports the Dwarf Sports Association, which helps people with dwarfism get into sports. She's a Brownie leader, an ambassador for the Scouting Association, and a campaigner for clean water for poor communities across the world. And Ellie's not giving up the sport she loves just yet. Despite five Paralympic golds, she's still hoping to win more medals.

Ellie winning gold at the Beijing Paralympic Games in 2008

JADE HAMEISTER

Polar explorer who skied to both poles

INSPIRED ON EVEREST

Jade Hameister was born in 2001 in Melbourne, Australia. Her parents loved the outdoors and Jade shared their sense of adventure and ambition.

Even so, it was a surprise when, aged thirteen, she announced at the dinner table that she wanted to ski to the South Pole. Jade had already proved she was tough. One year earlier, she had trekked to Everest Base Camp with her family and, while she was there, she'd met two female adventurers. One had climbed Mount Everest, the other had journeyed to the South Pole. Jade was so inspired. She wanted to have her own adventure!

GREENLAND CROSSING
(Expedition 2)
340 miles in 27 days

NORTH PO[LE]
(Expedition 1)
95 miles in 11 days

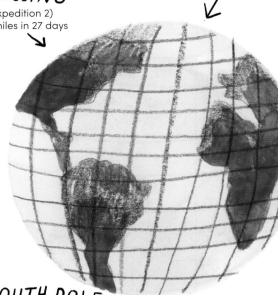

SOUTH POLE
(Expedition 3)
375 miles in 37 days

JADE HAMEISTER

> 66 YOU REALIZE WHAT YOU ONCE THOUGHT WERE YOUR LIMITS AREN'T YOUR LIMITS—AND THEN YOU REALIZE THERE REALLY AREN'T ANY LIMITS. 99

A POLAR QUEST

But there was a problem: you had to be sixteen to trek to the South Pole. Jade couldn't wait three years! She was old enough to attempt a trip to the North Pole and to cross Greenland on skis, so she decided to tackle these challenges while waiting for her sixteenth birthday. Then she'd ski to the South Pole. Jade was thinking big!

Training for these expeditions was essential. All her spare time was spent learning to ski and getting fit. She even dragged heavy tires across the beach to prepare for pulling a sledge across the snow.

Then, in April 2016, aged fourteen, Jade set off with her father on the ninety-five-mile journey to the North Pole. In freezing temperatures, she skied for over eight hours a day, dodging breaks in the ice and hungry polar bears, and dragging a sledge that weighed as much as she did.

It was tough going and she got painful frostbite. But she loved the adventure, and one of the best bits was sitting in her tent after a hard day, munching chips with her dad. After eleven days of skiing, they reached the Pole, making her one of the youngest people ever to do so.

Once they got home, Jade began planning her next trip. In June 2017, she attempted to cross 340 miles of the Greenland Ice Cap. The weather wasn't on her side—it was too warm! Jade got too hot in her polar outfit and her feet blistered in sweaty boots. Skiing was difficult because the ice had melted, so she smeared butter on her skis to make them extra slippy.

> **"OUT THERE YOU HAVE NOTHING, JUST THAT VOICE INSIDE YOUR HEAD—AND YOU CAN ACTUALLY LEARN FROM IT IF YOU LISTEN TO IT."**

Jade being presented with the Young Adventurer of the Year award in 2018 by Prince Harry, the Duke of Sussex

Each day was tougher than the last. Sometimes she wanted to give up but, incredibly, Jade dug deep and kept on going. She crossed Greenland in twenty-seven days and was the youngest woman ever to ski the distance without any help.

Now that Jade was sixteen, she could finally attempt the last leg of her polar quest: trekking 375 miles to the South Pole. It was the most demanding challenge so far. She crossed mountain ranges in blizzards, while dragging a heavy sledge behind her. She spent Christmas Day on the ice—her first ever white Christmas—and, after thirty-seven days, she made it to the South Pole.

SHAKING UP THE WORLD

Jade had become the youngest person ever to ski from the coast to the South Pole without any help, the youngest person to ski to both poles and to complete the "Polar Hat Trick." She hopes young women are inspired by her achievements and believes that they should focus on the possibilities of what they can do. And, for Jade, the possibilities are endless—once she finishes school, she's thinking about tackling Everest, or even space!

> **"IF IT WERE EASY, IT WOULDN'T BE AMAZING."**

SACHIN TENDULKAR

One of the greatest cricketers of all time

A BROTHER'S HELPING HAND

Sachin Tendulkar was born in 1973 in Mumbai, India. While he loved sports, he sometimes got into trouble at school so, to keep Sachin out of mischief, his parents encouraged him to start playing cricket, like his older brother.

When he was eleven, he went along to a practice session run by a famous cricket coach named Ramakant Achrekar. Ramakant could easily spot a talented player . . . but when it was Sachin's turn to bat, he kept missing the ball!

SACHIN RAMESH TENDULKAR

Sachin's brother explained that his little brother was very nervous. He asked if Ramakant would hide behind a tree so Sachin couldn't see him. He might be able to concentrate on hitting the ball if he didn't think he was being watched. Ramakant agreed, and Sachin started hitting the ball, hard. Straightaway, Ramakant knew Sachin was special.

Sachin started playing cricket three times a day—before, during, and after school. All this practicing made Sachin tired, so he would sometimes make mistakes batting. To keep him focused, his coach would place a coin on top of the wickets Sachin was defending. If he could stop bowlers knocking the coin off the wicket, Sachin would get to keep the money.

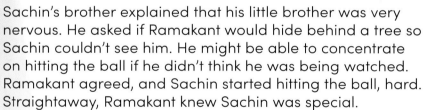

❝ DON'T STOP CHASING YOUR DREAMS BECAUSE DREAMS DO COME TRUE. ❞

"I WILL PLAY"

Sachin soon started playing for local Mumbai clubs and quickly began to score runs . . . a lot of runs. When he was twelve, he scored his first century, 100 runs, a great milestone in cricket. When he was fifteen, he scored a century every time he batted. In one game, he scored 326 runs! The other team was in tears because they couldn't knock the brilliant batsman's wickets over.

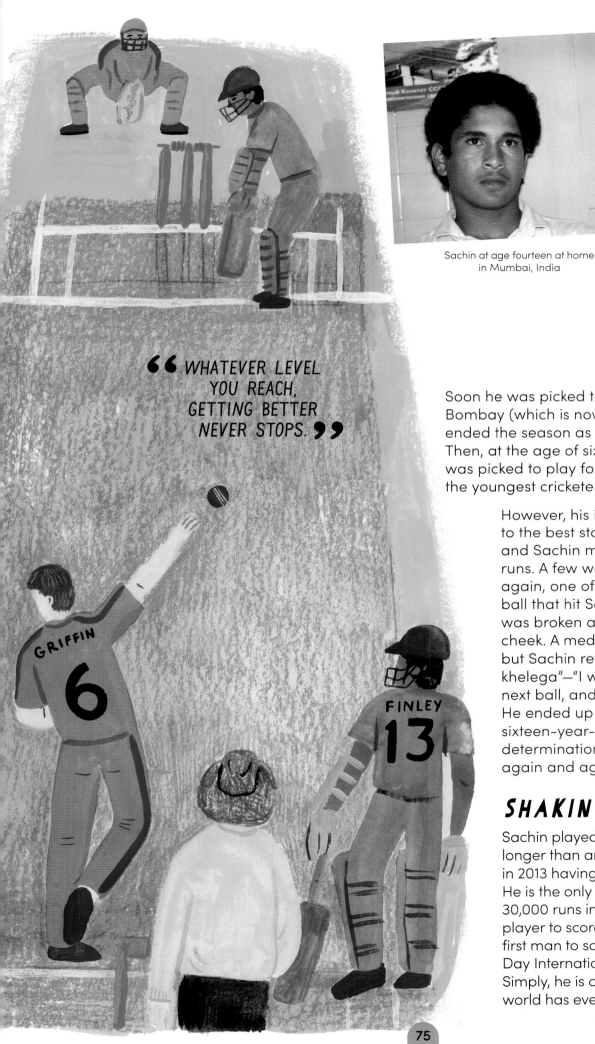

Sachin at age fourteen at home
in Mumbai, India

> **" WHATEVER LEVEL
> YOU REACH,
> GETTING BETTER
> NEVER STOPS. "**

Soon he was picked to play first-class cricket for Bombay (which is now known as Mumbai), and ended the season as Bombay's highest run scorer. Then, at the age of sixteen years and 205 days, he was picked to play for his country, and he is still the youngest cricketer ever to play for India.

However, his international career didn't get off to the best start. India was playing Pakistan and Sachin managed to score just fifteen runs. A few weeks later, playing Pakistan again, one of their fast bowlers bowled a ball that hit Sachin in the face. His nose was broken and he had a big cut across his cheek. A medic tried to help him off the field, but Sachin refused to leave. He said, "Main khelega"—"I will play"—lined up to face the next ball, and promptly hit it for four runs. He ended up saving the match. The sixteen-year-old had shown bravery and determination—qualities he would draw upon again and again in his cricketing career.

SHAKING UP THE WORLD

Sachin played for India for twenty-four years, longer than any other Indian cricketer, retiring in 2013 having broken record after record. He is the only player to have scored over 30,000 runs in international cricket, the only player to score 100 international centuries, the first man to score a double century in a One Day International match . . . the list goes on. Simply, he is one of the greatest batsmen the world has ever seen.

RED GERARD

BOARDING IN THE BACK GARDEN

Redmond, or Red, Gerard was born in 2000 in Ohio. He first tried snowboarding at the age of two and, being the sixth child in a family of seven children, he had to learn fast to keep up with his brothers and sisters.

When Red was seven, his family moved to the mountains of Colorado, where it was very snowy. In a field behind the new house, the family built jumps, dips, and rails into the deep snow. It was a snowboarder's paradise!

Red spent hours perfecting jumps and tricks. His older brother Brendan was already a professional snowboarder and helped Red improve his technique. Soon Red was way ahead of the other children his age.

> **"YOU FEEL THE WIND HITTING YOUR FACE AND THEN YOU LAND IT. AND THEN YOU THINK, 'OH MY GOSH, I WANT TO DO THAT AGAIN.' IT'S SO AWESOME."**

STARTING SLOPESTYLE

In 2008, at the age of eight, Red signed up for a local slopestyle competition. Slopestyle involves doing jumps and tricks down a snowboard run—just what he was doing in his back garden at home! Each rider gets three tries and the better the tricks, the more points they score.

Red did so well he entered more and more competitions and even got through to the National Championships, where all the best snowboarders in the country competed against one another. Unfortunately, on one of his runs in the Nationals, his helmet fell off, which meant he was automatically disqualified, or ruled out, from the competition.

But this was just the start of Red's racing. As he got older, he won bigger and better competitions. And when he was seventeen, he was selected for the US snowboarding team for the 2018 Winter Olympics in PyeongChang, South Korea. Red made the final of the Olympic slopestyle competition, but winning here wasn't going to be easy. . . .

SHAKING UP THE WORLD

On the morning of the final, Red overslept! Then he couldn't find his ski jacket and had to borrow a friend's. Finally, he made it to the start line, but on his first run he crashed out—not the best start! It didn't get much better. After all the finalists had had two runs, Red was in second to last place. If he was to win a medal, he was going to have to put in a superb final run.

Red was hoping to be one of the youngest medal winners ever

REDMOND "RED" GERARD

Red at the PyeongChang Winter Olympics in South Korea in 2018

> 66 I KIND OF LIKE THE FEELING OF LANDING MY RUN IN FRONT OF A CROWD. I LIKE TO SHOW OFF A LITTLE. 99

For round three, Red lined up his snowboard on the start line. He high-fived his teammates and set off downhill. He twisted and turned down the early part of the course, trying unusual jumps and tricks to gain more points. He knew he needed to finish with something special, though. With two jumps to go, he landed a 1080-degree twist—that's a jump spinning in the air three times! Then he attempted a massive backside triple cork 1440, spinning backward four times, while doing three head over heel flips. Amazingly, Red managed it, landing perfectly. His run sent him straight into first place and won him gold. At seventeen, Red became the youngest American ever to win an Olympic medal in snowboarding.

BETHANY HAMILTON

World-class champion surfer who survived a shark attack

SAND, SEA, AND SURF

Bethany Meilani Hamilton was born in 1990, the youngest of three children. She grew up on Kauai, an island of Hawaii which is famous for its big waves. Bethany's parents were keen surfers so Bethany was on a surfboard before she could even walk.

Very quickly, Bethany showed real skill and, by the age of eight, she had started winning local surf competitions. She knew if she practiced hard enough, she had the talent to become a professional surfer and would be able to enter competitions around the world.

But then, in 2003, everything changed.

HIDDEN DANGER

One October morning, Bethany was surfing off Kauai with her friends. Waiting for the next wave, she lay on her board, dangling her arms in the water, watching a family of turtles swim by. Then she felt a strange tug on her left arm. She thought nothing of it until she saw the sea around her turn blood red.

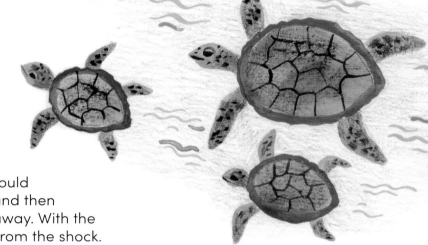

Bethany screamed. She'd been attacked by a tiger shark and now her whole arm was gone. She was in shock and losing a lot of blood and if she didn't get help soon, she would certainly die. Luckily, her friends quickly got her to shore, and then to a hospital, where the doctors operated on her straightaway. With the operation over, Bethany was left to sleep, and to recover from the shock.

Now, Bethany had to get used to life with just one arm. She had to relearn how to do all the things she had done before without thinking, like eating, getting dressed, and washing. But what Bethany wanted to do more than anything was get back on a surfboard.

On Thanksgiving Day, in November 2003, just one month after the attack, she hit the waves.

To begin with, it was tricky. Standing up and balancing was more difficult now because Bethany couldn't steady herself by holding both arms out, like she used to. She fell a few times, but she didn't give up and, with practice, she was soon surfing just as well as she had done before the attack. To help her paddle through the really big waves, her father fitted a special handle to her surfboard that she could grab on to as the waves hit.

> **"COURAGE DOESN'T MEAN YOU DON'T GET AFRAID. COURAGE MEANS YOU DON'T LET FEAR STOP YOU."**

BETHANY MEILANI HAMILTON

Bethany aged seventeen surfing in Phillip Island, Australia (above) and waving to fans at the 2019 Vans US Open of Surfing (left)

> **"I DON'T LOOK AT MYSELF AS 'DISABLED.'"**

SHAKING UP THE WORLD

Soon, Bethany was entering competitions again and, in 2004, she made the National Scholastic Surfing Association finals, coming fifth in the "18 and Under" category. It was an extraordinary comeback!

Bethany never stopped chasing her dream of surfing professionally and, by 2007, she was good enough to do just that. As such an inspiring role model, she has written a book about her life that has also been made into a film. Overcoming her challenges has also led her to set up a charity, Friends of Bethany, which helps people who have lost a limb. Bethany hates being called a shark-attack victim, as she doesn't consider herself to be one. She's not just a girl who survived a shark attack. She's not even just an impressive surfer with one arm. She's a completely fearless and amazing athlete!

TEMBA TSHERI

The youngest person to reach the top of the world

LIFE IN THE MOUNTAINS

Temba Tsheri Sherpa was born in Nepal in 1985. People who come from the mountainous Himalayan region of Nepal are called Sherpas, and Temba's father, like many other Sherpas, worked as a mountain expedition guide. Nine of the world's ten tallest mountains are found in the Himalayan region and Temba's father often spent weeks away from home, helping mountaineers scale the highest peaks in the world.

Temba loved listening to his father's stories of adventure. Climbing could be very dangerous, but he also found peace and beauty on the mountains. Soon, Temba had the mountaineering bug too, and his dream was to climb the biggest, and most dangerous, of them all: Mount Everest.

❝ EVEREST FOR ME IS BOTH A BEAUTY AND A BEAST. ❞

THE FIRST ATTEMPT

Everest has many hazards—deep ice crevasses, howling winds, and temperatures so cold fingers can freeze in minutes. But the 29,000-foot altitude is the most deadly thing about the mountain. This high up, there's very little oxygen in the air to breathe. Many climbers take bottled oxygen with them, but they still always feel out of breath and even putting on boots is exhausting.

At the age of fourteen, Temba signed up for an expedition to climb Everest. It was tough going, but his father and uncle traveled with him and encouraged him all the way. They spent weeks on the mountain, allowing their bodies to adjust to the altitude.

Finally, Temba was within reach of the summit. But the weather was so bad, he had to wait two days before he could attempt the final stretch.

This part of the mountain is known as the Death Zone, because the lack of oxygen often leaves people very confused. At one point, Temba took his gloves off to adjust his boots and forgot to put them back on. When he realized, forty-five minutes later, his hands had frozen solid. It was agony. Still, he courageously set off for the summit. But, just seventy feet from the top, with no oxygen and bad weather approaching, Temba realized it was too dangerous. He was brave enough to turn back.

> 66 ABOVE ALL, STRONG WILLPOWER, CONVICTION, AND DETERMINATION TO FULFILL YOUR DREAMS CAN TAKE YOU EVEN BEYOND EVEREST. 99

SHAKING UP THE WORLD

Once he got home, doctors decided five of Temba's frozen fingers were so badly damaged they needed to be removed. But even this didn't put Temba off. Just one year later, he joined another expedition and, in April 2001, aged fifteen, he set out again to reach his dream.

TEMBA TSHERI SHERPA

Bad weather meant progress was slow but, by May 23, the peak of the mountain was in sight once more. At midnight, the team began the last push for the summit. There was no stopping them this time and, seven hours later, Temba, together with a Spanish climber and another Sherpa, reached the top of the world. On the peak, Temba planted his school flag, the Nepalese flag, and a photo of Pasang Lhamu Sherpa, the first Nepalese woman to climb Everest. He spent only ten minutes up there, taking in his incredible achievement, before quickly heading back down to base camp.

When Temba arrived home, there was a huge crowd waiting to welcome him. Friends and family were joined by photographers and journalists wanting to hear the amazing story of the youngest person ever to scale Everest. He became a mountaineering hero!

Today, Temba still inspires mountaineers as he continues to climb and runs a trekking and adventure company. He trains aspiring young climbers, teaching them not just the technical skills, but also how to find the mental strength and courage that are needed to conquer Everest.

Temba back at school after his incredible climb (top) and prayer flags in front of Mount Everest (bottom)

NADIA COMĂNECI

First gymnast to score a perfect ten in the Olympic Games

CARTWHEELS IN THE PLAYGROUND

Nadia Comăneci was born in Romania in 1961. She was such an energetic little girl that when she was six, her mother signed her up for the local gymnastics school. She thought all the jumping around would wear Nadia out and make her a little calmer at home! As soon as she started lessons, it was clear Nadia was a natural.

One day, during playtime, six-year-old Nadia was practicing cartwheels when she was spotted by an important visitor to the school. He was the coach of the Romanian national gymnastics team and he visited schools across the country to find future stars. He thought Nadia had potential and invited her to train at his new gymnastics school.

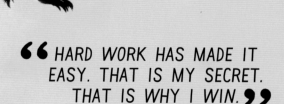

> HARD WORK HAS MADE IT EASY. THAT IS MY SECRET. THAT IS WHY I WIN.

The training regime was tough. Nadia practiced for six hours a day, five days a week, perfecting four different events. On the balance beam, Nadia had to learn how to jump and somersau on a wooden beam just four inches wide. Her floor exercises combined dance and acrobatics with music and when she tackled the vault, Nadia leaped from a springboard, twisting and turning high in the air. On the uneven bars, Nadia would swing between two high bars, performing spins, pirouettes, and somersaults. Each of these events needed incredible strength, split-second timing, and courage.

Nadia aged fifteen performing in the 1976 Montreal Olympic Games (right) and a year later at the International Gymnastics Tournament in London, England (below)

AN OUTSTANDING OLYMPICS

Nadia trained hard and she won her first national competition at the age of ten. Then, in 1975, she won more gold medals in her first major European competition. But her biggest test was yet to come. She was selected for the Romanian Olympic Team and would compete at the Montreal Olympics in 1976. She would be just fourteen years old!

At the Olympics, Nadia was a sensation. The whole world watched in amazement as this young Romanian girl performed with extraordinary skill and precision. The crowd fell silent and the pressure was on as Nadia leaped onto the uneven bars and performed a dazzling, flawless routine. Not one of the judges could fault it: she got a perfect score. For the first time ever, a gymnast at the Olympic Games had scored a perfect 10!

> " I DON'T RUN AWAY FROM A CHALLENGE BECAUSE I AM AFRAID. I RUN TOWARD IT BECAUSE THE ONLY WAY TO ESCAPE FEAR IS TO TRAMPLE IT BENEATH YOUR FEET. "

Except there was a problem. The official scoreboard wasn't programed to show such a high score. The highest number it could display was 9.99, so a 10.00 had to be shown as 1.00! Nadia was confused, but a judge explained, and the crowd soon went wild!

She went on to get six more perfect tens in the Olympics, winning three gold medals, one silver, and one bronze.

SHAKING UP THE WORLD

Nadia was the star of the Olympics. Her picture was on magazine covers across the world and she returned to Romania a hero. Four years later, at the Moscow Olympics, Nadia hit the heights again, winning two gold and two silver medals. She retired from competing in 1984 and started coaching, working with the Romanian junior gymnastics team before eventually leaving Romania and moving to the United States.

With her confidence and creativity, she was named one of the best athletes of the twentieth century and she was the second person to be inducted into the International Gymnastics Hall of Fame. Nadia's achievements were extraordinary, inspiring millions of young athletes and changing the sport forever.

NADIA COMĂNECI

ROMANIA

BILLY MONGER

Motorsports rising star

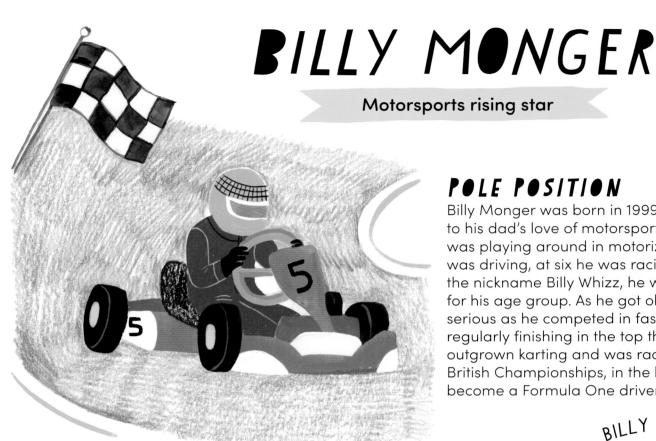

POLE POSITION

Billy Monger was born in 1999 in Surrey in the UK. Thanks to his dad's love of motorsports, it wasn't long before Billy was playing around in motorized go-karts. At three he was driving, at six he was racing, and by ten, and with the nickname Billy Whizz, he was British Kart Champion for his age group. As he got older, the racing got more serious as he competed in faster and faster go-karts, regularly finishing in the top three. By 2016, he had outgrown karting and was racing in the Formula Four British Championships, in the hope that, one day, he would become a Formula One driver.

Formula One is the fastest motor-racing sport in the world. Teams battle it out over a season, collecting points by racing on motor circuits across twenty-one countries. Formula Four cars are single-seat machines, just like Formula One cars and, although a little less powerful, they can still reach speeds of over 125 miles per hour! Racing these cars takes skill and nerve and seventeen-year-old Billy seemed to have bags of both.

HORROR ON THE TRACK

In April 2017, in his second year of Formula Four racing, Billy was competing at Donington Park circuit. He got off to a good start, but the race ended horrifically when Billy was involved in a terrible accident. It was so bad, Billy ended up having to have both his legs amputated.

Almost immediately, Billy's racing team began raising money to help with his recovery. Many of Billy's Formula One heroes, including Jenson Button and Lewis Hamilton, donated money and in twenty-four hours over $600,000 was raised.

BILLY MONGER

But Billy didn't feel sorry for himself. Instead, he set about overcoming this new challenge in his life with the same grit and determination he had shown on the racetrack. Within months, he had artificial legs fitted and was learning to walk again. But he wanted to do more than walk. His dream was still to become a Formula One driver: he wanted to race again.

❝I DON'T SEE HOW BEING UPSET FOREVER IS GOING TO MAKE A DIFFERENCE.❞

"MY ACCIDENT CHANGED MY LIFE, BUT IT WON'T DEFINE IT."

But there was a problem. Disabled drivers aren't allowed to race single-seater cars according to motorsports rules. Billy appealed to the International Automobile Federation, or FIA, the group that decides the motor-racing guidelines and, after months of discussions, they agreed to let Billy race again, only not in a regular Formula Four car.

A friend invited him to visit the headquarters of Carlin, a local motorsports team, and they began building a specially adapted machine for Billy to drive. They added levers to the steering wheel, so he could adjust his speed with his hands instead of his feet, and they altered the brake pedal, so he could use a specially designed "racing" leg to slow down. Soon he was test-driving the new car and hitting speeds of over 100 miles per hour.

Billy about to drive the specially adapted car made just for him

Billy with one of his motorsport heroes, Lewis Hamilton

"BILLY WHIZZ IS BACK I GUESS!"

SHAKING UP THE WORLD

In March 2018, less than a year after his crash, Billy started racing for Carlin, not in Formula Four, but in Formula Three, a tougher, faster competition. In his first race, at Oulton Park, he came in third—a podium finish! By the end of the season, he'd managed pole position—that's first position—not once, but twice, along with three podium places, finishing sixth overall. Not bad for his first season back behind the wheel.

Billy has shown incredible bravery, dedication, and courage to climb back into the driver's seat, and all with a big smile on his face. He's astounded the whole motorsports community with his "can-do" attitude. Now he's concentrating on getting even faster, so that he's on the right track to achieve his Formula One racing dream.

POCAHONTAS

Native American princess who kept the peace

UNWELCOME VISITORS

Pocahontas was a Native American girl born around 1596 in what is now the state of Virginia. Her father was an important leader called Chief Powhatan, who ruled over thirty different Native American tribes.

In May 1607, when Pocahontas was twelve, three great ships arrived near her village. On board were English explorers, led by Captain John Smith. They had been sailing for weeks and wanted to come ashore to rest and pick up supplies. Chief Powhatan gave them permission but, shortly after they landed, the sailors began building a big fort. It was clear they were beginning to set up a colony, a place where more and more English and European people, called settlers, would come to live.

The chief didn't want the settlers to stay. He led a group of his people to try to force them off his land, but they were driven back. The Native Americans had arrows and knives, but the English had muskets and cannons and armor. Powhatan realized he had to find another way of beating the invaders.

RISKING HER LIFE

Some days later, John Smith was out exploring when he was captured by Powhatan's men and dragged before their leader. He believed he was going to be beaten by Native Americans with wooden clubs . . . maybe even killed. But before the punishment could begin, a young girl standing by Powhatan's side rushed over and laid her head on Smith's. If Smith was going to die, she would die too.

That girl was Pocahontas, Powhatan's daughter. Powhatan saw how brave his daughter was, risking her life for this stranger. So the chief agreed to release the Englishman unharmed. Smith was free to return to his camp but there was one condition: he and Pocahontas had to become friends.

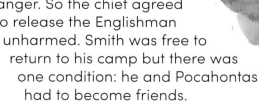

So Pocahontas visited Smith regularly in the settlers' camp. When they weren't chatting and learning each other's language, she would play with the children there, showing them how to do cartwheels and handstands.

POCAHONTAS

By saving Smith's life she had brought the two sides together and stopped people from dying in battle.

When Smith returned to England in 1609 after he was hurt in an accident, Pocahontas stopped visiting the English settlers. Without their special relationship keeping the two sides together, the fighting began again. Four years later, when some Native Americans captured a group of settlers and stole their weapons, the other settlers came up with a plan to kidnap Pocahontas. They thought her father might set the English prisoners free in exchange for his daughter.

A painting by Jean Leon Gerome Ferris showing how he imagined Pocahontas may have looked

The plan almost worked. The prisoners were released, but Chief Powhatan kept their weapons. In return, the settlers kept Pocahontas. While she was a prisoner, Pocahontas learned all about the English way of life. She met another settler, John Rolfe, and, by 1616, they were married with a son. Their marriage helped stop the fighting between the English and Native Americans, and the years after became known as the Peace of Pocahontas.

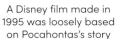

A Disney film made in 1995 was loosely based on Pocahontas's story

❝ IT IS POCAHONTAS TO WHOM MY HEARTY AND BEST THOUGHTS ARE, AND HAVE BEEN A LONG TIME SO ENTANGLED. ❞

John Rolfe

SHAKING UP THE WORLD

When people in England heard of the marriage, they were desperate to see the girl who had stolen an Englishman's heart. In May 1616, Pocahontas traveled to England and spent almost a year traveling around, even meeting the king. But as she was getting ready to go back home, she fell ill and died at the age of twenty-one.

The story of Pocahontas has been told again and again in paintings, books, and films. Whether it's her bravery in saving Smith's life, or her kindness getting to know new people from another land, Pocahontas is remembered as a strong young woman whose courage and love brought people together.

POCAHONTAS

HECTOR PIETERSON

AN UNEQUAL LIFE

Hector Pieterson was born in Soweto in South Africa in 1963. Back then, the government had very strict rules about what Hector was allowed to do, where he was allowed to go, and who he was allowed to meet. That's because Hector was black and, in South Africa at the time, the white government treated black people as second-class citizens. They tried to make black and white people live and work separately from each other and this system was called apartheid.

Black people weren't allowed to run businesses, own lots of land, or marry white people. They weren't allowed to use the same swimming pools, toilets, or buses. Black families were also forced to live in certain areas, like Soweto, which were on the edges of towns and cities and often had only very basic living conditions, with poor water and electricity supplies. These places were called townships.

" GROWING UP, EVEN THOUGH WE HEARD ABOUT APARTHEID IT DID NOT MAKE SENSE TO US BECAUSE THERE IS NO WHITE PERSON IN SOWETO. THE ONLY WHITE PERSON THAT YOU'D SEE WOULD BE SUPERINTENDENT, POLICE. **"**

Antoinette Sithole, Hector's sister

Hector was an intelligent, cheerful boy with lots of friends. He loved karate and, like many boys his age, he loved to tease his classmates and play practical jokes. He was known by his nicknames, Beans or Chopper. His school was very crowded. They didn't have many books and the teachers were not paid very much money. It was as if the white government didn't want children like Hector to get a good education.

In 1976, the government demanded that children in township schools be taught in Afrikaans, the language of white South Africa. The students in Soweto felt this was another way of making learning difficult for them. The government didn't care that they were unhappy. They said if black pupils didn't want to learn in Afrikaans, they shouldn't bother going to school.

A FIGHT FOR EDUCATION

In May that year, students and teachers in Soweto went on strike to protest the changes. They planned a demonstration march on June 16. Although Hector was only twelve, he wanted to join his older sister Antoinette at the march.

The protest began peacefully enough, but then the police arrived. They were determined to stop the students' demonstration by blocking their path. The crowd soon became anxious and some people started throwing stones at the police. The police fired tear gas right back at the students. Tear gas stings the eyes and makes it difficult to see, so people started to panic. As the crowd began to run away, the gunshots started. The police were firing at the students.

> 66 EVERYBODY WAS JUST SHOOTING AT RANDOM. I SAW A LITTLE BOY FALL DOWN. 99
>
> *Sam Nzima, a photographer*

It was very dangerous on the streets of Soweto during the protests in 1976 (top) and children at the Hector Pieterson Memorial and Museum (right)

HECTOR PIETERSON

SHAKING UP THE WORLD

Hector was one of the first to be hit. He fell to the ground but was scooped up by another protestor, Mbuyisa Makhubo, who tried to find help. Hector was rushed to a hospital, but it was too late. He was one of around 170 students who died at the protest. The horrific image of Mbuyisa carrying Hector, with Antoinette running helplessly alongside, was captured by news photographer Sam Nzima. The picture symbolizes the terror the children felt that day.

The photograph shocked the world. People questioned how a government could allow their police to behave this way. It didn't stop apartheid in South Africa straightaway, but Hector's death drew attention to the way the country was ruled, and apartheid was finally stopped in 1994.

Hector has never been forgotten in South Africa. There is a memorial and museum in his name and every June, on the anniversary of his death, the country celebrates Youth Day. It's a day for South Africans to be reminded of their past, while looking to their future.

89

SAMANTHA SMITH

The girl who wanted Russia and America to be friends

ON THE BRINK OF WAR

Samantha Reed Smith was born in 1972 in Houlton, Maine. When she was growing up, the two world superpowers, America and the Soviet Union (or USSR), were great enemies.

Although they weren't fighting each other, each superpower built up great armies and even greater stocks of weapons in case war did break out. Each believed that if they had enough powerful weapons, such as nuclear missiles that could kill millions of people, their enemy would be too scared to attack them. Many people, including Samantha, were worried, because if the Soviet Union or America fired these missiles, it would start a terrible war.

Samantha's mother suggested she write to the leader of the Soviet Union, Yury Andropov, to ask if he was planning to attack the US or not. Samantha decided to do just that and she sent a letter in the mail. Some months later, having received no response, she wrote again. This time, soon after, an envelope arrived for her. It was a reply from Yury Andropov himself!

> **THE WHOLE THING STARTED WHEN I ASKED MY MOTHER IF THERE WAS GOING TO BE A WAR.**

AN UNUSUAL INVITATION

In his letter, Andropov said that the Soviet Union was doing everything it could to prevent another war. He wrote about how, after the Second World War, Soviet people wanted to live in peace with their neighbors. They wanted to grow crops, invent things, write books, and explore space. He said that although they had nuclear weapons he would never fire them first. He also invited Samantha and her family to visit.

Samantha with her parents, Jane and Arthur, visiting Red Square in Moscow in 1983

Because America and the USSR were so afraid of each other, very few Americans visited the Soviet Union and hardly any Soviet people went to America. But in July 1983, Samantha bravely accepted Andropov's invitation and flew to the Soviet capital, Moscow, with her family. For a week, she was shown the sights. She was amazed by the subway stations with chandeliers hanging from the ceilings and beautiful paintings decorating the walls. She met a female astronaut, visited the circus, enjoyed the ballet, and was given beautiful gifts. Then Samantha spent a week at a children's camp on the Black Sea, where she shared a dormitory with nine other girls and spent her time swimming, dancing, and learning the Russian language.

Her every move was followed by journalists, who told her story in newspapers around the world. Grown-ups in America and the USSR realized they weren't so different after all when they saw an eleven-year-old American girl meeting and playing with Soviet children.

> **"I THINK THAT KIDS AND GROWN-UPS ALL OVER THE WORLD ARE LIKE A GREAT BIG FAMILY, AND WE HAVE TO FIND A WAY TO LIVE TOGETHER."**

Samantha and her parents exploring the Grand Kremlin Palace, with its magnificent chandeliers

SHAKING UP THE WORLD

When Samantha arrived home, life became very busy. She had become so popular that people wanted her to make television programs about politics and speak at meetings about peace. In December 1983, she spoke at a conference in Japan and suggested that US and Soviet leaders swap granddaughters for two weeks every year because they wouldn't want to bomb a country that their granddaughter was visiting.

"WHAT WOULD YOU LIKE TO WISH ALL CHILDREN?"

> **TO LIVE WITHOUT WORRYING ABOUT WAR.**

She was even asked to start acting in a television series. It was while returning home from some filming in 1985 that the plane she was on crashed, and tragically Samantha and her father were killed. Both the US president, Ronald Reagan, and the new Soviet leader, Mikhail Gorbachev, sent letters of sympathy to Samantha's mother.

After her death, a statue of Samantha was put up in her hometown and the Soviet Union released a stamp with her picture. She had a tulip, a diamond, a ship, a school, a mountain, and even an asteroid named after her. Samantha's mother was determined to continue what Samantha had started so she set up a charity dedicated to educating children about peace and international friendship.

SAMANTHA REED SMITH

CLAUDETTE COLVIN

BLACK IN ALABAMA

A fifteen-year-old Claudette, when she was in tenth grade in high school

Claudette Colvin was born in 1939 in Montgomery, Alabama. She was a confident and hard-working young girl, quiet, well mannered, and intelligent. When Ms. Nesbitt, her tenth-grade teacher, asked her what she wanted to be when she grew up, she replied, "President of the United States."

But at that time in Alabama and other southern states of America, there were laws that kept white and Black people apart. Officially, they were "separate but equal" but everyone knew that Black people were treated very unfairly. And as a Black American, that made Claudette angry.

> 66 THERE WAS SEGREGATION EVERYWHERE. THE CHURCHES, BUSES, AND SCHOOLS WERE ALL SEGREGATED AND YOU COULDN'T EVEN GO TO THE SAME RESTAURANTS. 99

White and Black people were born in separate hospitals, went to separate schools, and even watched movies in separate theaters. But one place where they were together was on the buses. Buses had special rules, though: the ten rows of seats at the front were for white people; Black people had to sit at the back. If all the seats at the front were taken, the driver would order Black people to stand up to let more white people sit down.

TAKING A STAND

On March 2, 1955, fifteen-year-old Claudette finished school as usual and caught the bus home with her friends. The four girls sat in a row, two on either side of the aisle, with Claudette by the window. The bus got busier and soon all the seats for white people were taken, so when a white passenger got on, there was nowhere for her to sit. Quickly, Claudette's three friends stood up to let the lady sit down, but Claudette didn't move.

CLAUDETTE COLVIN

At school that week, Claudette had been learning all about the slave trade. Africans and Black Americans had been slaves in the South until the trade was ended less than a hundred years earlier. Claudette had read about Black heroes like Harriet Tubman and Sojourner Truth who had helped slaves escape their owners and fought for change. That day, Claudette wanted change too.

> **"I COULD NOT MOVE BECAUSE HISTORY HAD GLUED ME TO THE SEAT."**

There were now three spare seats on the bus, but the white lady would not sit down. Black people and white people could not even share the same row. The bus driver yelled at Claudette to move, but she still did not get up. He called two policemen over and they demanded she move. Again, she refused. Claudette knew she was in serious trouble, but she wanted to make a stand by staying seated.

The two policemen dragged her off the bus. Her schoolbooks flew everywhere. Claudette was very frightened, as white policemen had been known to beat up Black people—even children. They put her in handcuffs and took her to the police station. She was alone and scared.

When Claudette's mother heard what had happened, she rushed to the police station to see her daughter. After paying some money, she was allowed to take Claudette home. By now, news of the brave girl had spread around the Black community, and her neighbors and friends lined the streets in support as she drove past.

> **"I WAS TIRED OF HOPING FOR JUSTICE. WHEN MY MOMENT CAME, I WAS READY."**

SHAKING UP THE WORLD

Claudette's protest was followed by more demonstrations. Nine months after Claudette, Rosa Parks was also arrested for not giving up her seat on a bus. Then, inspired by Claudette and Rosa, thousands of Black people refused to use the city's bus system until things changed. Over a year later, making people sit separately on public transportation was finally made illegal.

Claudette's bravery helped make things fairer for Black people across America. It encouraged more people to support the civil rights movement, until, eventually, segregation was brought to an end.

IQBAL MASIH

The child slave brave enough to make a stand

SOLD INTO SLAVERY

Iqbal Masih was born in a small village in Pakistan in 1983. His parents didn't have much money and one day, when Iqbal was around four, they sold him for $12 to a man who owned a carpet factory. Sadly, selling a child wasn't that unusual in this part of Pakistan—it was known as debt slavery—but it was still very cruel.

Every morning at 4:00 a.m., men would collect Iqbal from his home to take him to the factory. Along with other children, he was made to work a loom, a machine for weaving carpets, for twelve hours a day, seven days a week. Iqbal made beautiful silk carpets, but it was hot and tiring work and the men treated the young workers terribly. Iqbal decided he had to escape.

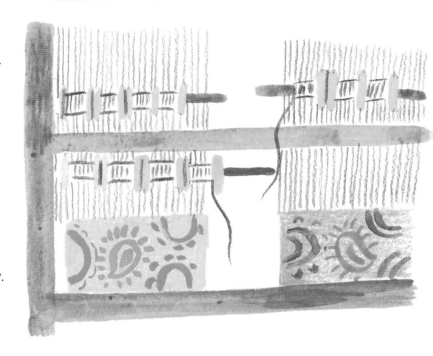

A DARING ESCAPE

One day, when the factory guards weren't looking, Iqbal managed to sneak out. He ran to a police station and asked for help, but the police took him straight back to the factory, where he was punished for running away and chained to his loom.

❝ CHILDREN SHOULD HAVE PENS IN THEIR HANDS NOT TOOLS. ❞

A young boy working a loom in a carpet factory, just like the one Iqbal was forced to work in

By the time Iqbal was ten, the owner had stopped chaining him up. He'd spent half his life working in the factory. He had to try to break free again. One afternoon, when the guards were napping in the hot sun, Iqbal crept past them. But where should he go? The police wouldn't help and if he returned home, he would quickly be found. He had no choice. He had to live on the streets. It was tough, but at least he had escaped the factory.

While he was on the streets, Iqbal heard of a group that was trying to stop debt slavery and help children just like him. The group arranged for Iqbal to go to school and promised he would never have to return to the factory. Now Iqbal could play, make friends, and learn, all the things most children do every day, but which Iqbal had never been able to do before.

SHAKING UP THE WORLD

Iqbal was now free, but he wanted to help his friends who were still in slavery. He started campaigning, speaking at demonstrations about his experiences, and even sneaking into factories to talk to other slave children. He was such a passionate speaker, everyone listened, and soon articles about him started appearing in newspapers and magazines.

IQBAL MASIH

"WE ARE FREE!"

A young Iqbal (top) and the special group, named the Bonded Labour Liberation Front, that campaigns against slavery and helped Iqbal return to school (bottom)

The fight against child labor grew and the cruel carpet makers had to take notice. Iqbal helped over 3,000 children break free. He wanted to help thousands more, but the factory owners were angry with what Iqbal was doing. Child labor was cheap, so they made big profits. If they couldn't use children anymore, they would lose money.

One day in 1995, Iqbal was at home with his family, playing with some friends on a bike, when gunshots rang out. Someone had shot and killed Iqbal. The crime wasn't investigated properly, but many believed it must have been angry factory owners wanting Iqbal dead.

People around the world were shocked and wondered how such a thing could happen. But those who knew him, had heard him speak, or believed in his cause were determined not to forget him. He was a hero with extraordinary passion, who inspired thousands to find freedom, and groups set up in his name continued his fight against child slavery.

Unfortunately, child labor still goes on in Pakistan and many other countries around the world, but Iqbal was brave enough to tell his story as part of the fight to stamp it out.

THANDIWE CHAMA

Zambian educational rights activist

A SCHOOL WITHOUT TEACHERS

Thandiwe Chama was born in 1991 in Lusaka, the capital of Zambia. At that time, many people in Zambia had contracted a disease called AIDS. AIDS is caused by a virus known as HIV, or human immunodeficiency virus, which attacks the parts of the body that fight disease. It means even the most common bugs can be deadly, and when Thandiwe was growing up, it was very difficult to treat.

Thandiwe lived in a poor part of Lusaka where, because so many people had died of the disease, there weren't enough workers to fill all the jobs across the city. Many schools had to close down, including Thandiwe's. Thandiwe had studied hard at school and was one of the best students in her class. She wanted a good education to help her and her family escape poverty but knew that if she couldn't go to school, she would never learn to read or write and would never get a good job.

❝ WE ARE THE VOICE FOR THE VOICELESS. ❞

Thandiwe was determined to continue her education but knew she would have to find a way to do this herself. She persuaded her friends at school to join her in a protest and led them on a march to find a school that was still running so they could demand an education. When the sixty pupils arrived at the new school, Thandiwe insisted they be allowed to go to lessons there. The teachers were so impressed with Thandiwe's leadership and the children's commitment, they agreed to let them stay. This was Thandiwe's first step toward change.

❝ OUR AIM IS TO MAKE SURE EVERY CHILD IN THE WORLD HAS BEEN HEARD. ❞

Thandiwe's hometown, Lusaka, the capital city of Zambia

DEMANDING MORE CHANGE

It was great to be back at school, but there were still problems. Parts of the school building had no roof and many windows were missing. In the summer, sitting in the hot sun made learning difficult and in the winter the pupils would get wet in the rain. Thandiwe met with important people from the government to ask for their help. Soon they had new classrooms, a science lab, and computers! She even persuaded local businesses to pay for a library, so that anyone, no matter how poor, could borrow books to read.

> **" IF CHILDREN ARE GIVEN AN OPPORTUNITY, THEY FOR SURE CAN CONTRIBUTE IN MAKING THIS WORLD A BETTER PLACE. "**

She understood that every child needed to learn how to read, write, and do math, but Thandiwe also realized that they needed to know more about AIDS if this dreadful disease was to be stopped.

She started giving talks at local churches, to teach people how to protect against it. She explained how important it was to be checked by doctors and went with children to be tested at health clinics if their parents couldn't take them. She even wrote a children's book, *The Chicken with AIDS*, to teach young children about AIDS and HIV.

SHAKING UP THE WORLD

In 2007, when Thandiwe was sixteen, she was awarded the International Children's Peace Prize for her work in fighting for children's rights. She discovered that many more people would now listen to what she had to say, so she campaigned even harder. She began traveling the world, speaking at conferences about the difficulties that children experience all over Africa.

Then Thandiwe helped set up KidsRights Youngsters with other winners of the Children's Peace Prize. It's a movement that fights for rights, education, healthcare, gender equality, and youth leadership for young people across the world. Today, Thandiwe is still campaigning and, thanks to her, many children now have brighter futures.

THANDIWE CHAMA

KIMMIE WEEKS

Liberian children's rights activist

ESCAPING THE REBELS

Kimmie Weeks was born in 1981 in Monrovia, the capital of Liberia in West Africa. As a little boy, life was good, but when he was nine years old, his world was turned upside down. Different political parties began fighting to take control of Liberia and soon rebels armed with guns roamed the country. They were heading for Kimmie's city, hoping to bring down the president and his army.

The center of Monrovia in Liberia, West Africa, where Kimmie was born

KIMMIE WEEKS

66 WHERE THERE'S LIFE, THERE'S HOPE. 99

Across Liberia, hospitals, schools, shops, and offices all closed as people fled their homes to escape the fighting. Kimmie and his mom escaped too and found themselves living in an old school building, hiding from the rebels. For months, sixteen families made one classroom their home. There was no water or electricity, and as Kimmie lay on the floor at night he could hear the constant crack of gunfire from fighting nearby.

But for Kimmie, the most shocking thing about the war was that many of the soldiers he saw were young boys just like him. The political leaders had forced boys and girls as young as six to take up guns and fight. This was no game. This was the real thing.

Soon, with no fresh water and no medicine, disease swept through the school building. Kimmie became very ill with cholera, and lay on his bed, barely awake, for days. But, incredibly, just as everyone thought Kimmie had died, he began to get better. He believed he'd been given another chance, and promised to spend the rest of his life helping disadvantaged children.

VOICE OF THE FUTURE

After a few years, the situation in Liberia got a little better when other African countries came to help. Kimmie's health improved too and before long it was safe enough to return home. But Kimmie and his mother found little left of their house. Their city had been destroyed and many of Kimmie's friends had been killed in the war. He was so desperate for life to improve, he began volunteering at his local hospital, caring for sick and poor children. In 1994, he set up an organization, Voice of the Future, that helped children across the country get access to proper healthcare and education. He was determined to help get his country back on its feet.

> ❝ EACH AND EVERY PERSON CAN DO SOMETHING TO SAVE A LIFE. ❞

But Kimmie hadn't forgotten the child soldiers he'd once seen. During the war in Liberia, 20,000 children were forced to fight. So, in 1996, at the age of fifteen, Kimmie founded the Children's Disarmament Campaign to fight against rebel leaders using children as soldiers. He gave lots of talks and interviews and wrote articles for newspapers. It didn't take long for the world to take notice of Kimmie's message.

However, the president of Liberia still wanted to use children in his army and now Kimmie was making it very difficult. As a result, the Liberian government tried to have Kimmie killed. Kimmie had to go into hiding to save his own life, so he escaped the country and flew to America.

> ❝ I REMAIN A STRONG BELIEVER IN THE POWER OF YOUNG PEOPLE TO MAKE CHANGE HAPPEN. ❞

Kimmie today (top) and Kimmie regularly visits Liberia and campaigns for children affected by war (bottom)

SHAKING UP THE WORLD

As a refugee in the US, Kimmie continued his campaigning, giving children affected by war opportunities they wouldn't have had before. And today, he travels the world, sharing his experiences and shining a light on the horrors of child soldiers. And with a new president in Liberia, it's also now safe for him to go back home, where his work has been recognized and rewarded. In 2007, he was awarded the highest honor possible, becoming a Knight Grand Commander, the youngest person to ever receive this honor in Liberia.

MAYRA AVELLAR NEVES

Campaigner who risked her life for an education

TOO SCARED TO PLAY

Mayra Avellar Neves was born in 1990 in Rio de Janeiro, one of the biggest cities in Brazil. Mayra grew up in a very poor area of Rio, known as a favela or a slum. Crime was everywhere in the favela and gunfights between rival gangs or the police happened almost every day. When Mayra heard the loud gunshots, she would hide under her bed, too scared to come out, and it was far too dangerous to play outside.

One day, Mayra went along to a neighborhood meeting organized by a charity trying to improve lives in the favela. There she learned that without an education a child was more likely to turn to a life of crime, but if that child learned to read and write, they would be able to get a job and improve their situation.

The favela in Rio de Janeiro where Mayra grew up

❝ ALL CHILDREN SHOULD HAVE A SAFE UPBRINGING AND THE RIGHT TO AN EDUCATION. ❞

THE COURAGE TO PROTEST

But getting an education was difficult. There was so much violence on the streets, children were risking their lives just walking to school, and people who traveled into the favela to work, like teachers and doctors, stopped coming.

Mayra was desperate to continue her lessons. She found a school outside the favela and persuaded them to let her attend. It was very different from the school she was used to. There wasn't much crime in the neighborhood and inside the school it was calm. Mayra was happy here and it made her think. Why couldn't all children go to a school like this?

❝ I WANT TO TELL PEOPLE THAT EVEN THOUGH THEY DON'T HAVE MONEY, THEY CAN STAND UP FOR THEIR RIGHTS. ❞

MAYRA AVELLAR NEVES

So, in 2002, Mayra organized a protest march through her favela called Peace March Against Violence. She wanted the criminal gangs and police to pay attention.

Two hundred children, all dressed in white, joined in. Mayra was worried because they marched through some risky areas, but luckily nobody got hurt. And, the march was a success: a cease-fire was agreed to, which meant the gangs and police stopped fighting so children could go to school safely. Mayra learned a big lesson that day—standing up for her rights could make a difference.

> **❝ I WANT TO SHOW WHAT WE CAN ACHIEVE, NOT WHAT WE CAN'T ACHIEVE. I REFUSE TO ACCEPT THIS LEVEL OF VIOLENCE AND BELIEVE IT CAN CHANGE. ❞**

While many people supported Mayra, there were many more who believed nothing would, or could change. Mayra wanted to convince these people that life could be better in the favela. The following year, Mayra organized another march—the Walk for Peace. She wanted Brazilians across the country to understand that people living in the favelas deserved education, healthcare, and peace, just like every other Brazilian.

More than 300 young people from Mayra's favela joined her Walk for Peace, asking for less violence between gangs and the police

SHAKING UP THE WORLD

The Walk for Peace was much bigger than Mayra's first demonstration, and it sent a strong message to the rest of the country. She started organizing regular neighborhood meetings to get people working together and, slowly, as community spirit grew, people in the favela realized change was possible.

Mayra's brave actions were recognized, both in Brazil, where the government was forced to improve living conditions in the favelas, and also across the globe. In 2008, she was awarded the International Children's Peace Prize and was invited to speak about children's rights around the world.

The Brazilian favelas are still dangerous places. But Mayra continues to campaign for the right to safety, giving children in a poor and extremely violent environment hope and opportunities for the future.

NEHA GUPTA

Determined to help the disadvantaged have a better life

VISITING THE GRANDPARENTS

Neha Gupta was born in New Zealand in 1996 but moved to the US when she was three. Her parents grew up in India, where they had a special family tradition—every year on family birthdays, Neha's parents and grandparents would visit the orphanage in their town and celebrate with the children there. An orphanage is a home for orphans, or children who don't have parents to look after them, so Neha's family would bring gifts and food to share. It was always a happy day, which also reminded the Guptas of how lucky they were to have their family. Even when Neha's parents had left India, they continued to visit the orphanage once a year.

When Neha was around five, she started joining her parents on their trips to the orphanage in India. She soo got to know the children who lived there, and it wasn't long before she discovered how difficult their lives were Some of the children even had to sleep on the floor!

Neha thought about what it must be like to live there—to have no family to make sure she was safe, no school, and no chance of seeing a doctor if she became unwell It made her very sad, and she wanted to do as much as she could to help.

> **❝ ONCE I TURNED MY EMPATHY INTO ACTION IT OPENED MY EYES TO THE FULFILLMENT ONE RECEIVES BY HELPING OTHERS. ❞**

EMPOWERING ORPHANS

Once Neha had returned home, she set about raising money. She organized a neighborhood secondhand sale, selling her own toys, homemade gifts, and greeting cards, which raised over $800. Encouraged, she kept going, and by the time she returned to India one year later, she had over $5,000 to spend on food, clothes, blankets, and books for the children.

But Neha didn't stop at secondhand sales. She got in touch with big companies and persuaded them to donate money to her cause. Over the next few years, Neha raised over $1.5 million dollars and helped over 25,000 disadvantaged children, both in India and closer to home in America. At the age of nine, Neha set up her own company, Empower Orphans, to help raise and spend the money, and has provided five libraries, four computer labs for underfunded schools, a well to provide clean water to a village in India, and medical and dental care for thousands.

SHAKING UP THE WORLD

But Neha also realized that it was important for the orphans to be able to help themselves. She arranged for some of them to be taught how to use sewing machines. She thought if they learned a practical skill, they could use it to earn money when they were older, and she was right—many of these children went on to become seamstresses and tailors.

> **ONE PERSON HAS POWER AND CAN MAKE A DIFFERENCE IN THE WORLD.**

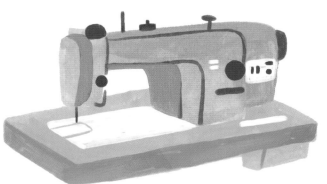

NEHA GUPTA

Neha being given the International Children's Peace Prize in 2014

One year, when Neha returned to her grandparents' village, she met a woman who had attended her sewing course. The money she earned from sewing meant she could now afford to pay for electricity in her home. Thanks to electric lights, her brother could now study in the evenings, which meant he was able to get a better job. Neha calls this the "ripple effect," where one good thing leads to lots of other good things, and she wants to see it happen again and again.

For Neha's drive to improve the lives of orphans, she was awarded a gold US President's Volunteer Service Award in 2011 and, three years later, won the International Children's Peace Prize. Today, all the incredible fundraising she has done means that others are in a position to thrive and generate their own ripple effect.

EMMA GONZÁLEZ

SHOCK AT SCHOOL

Emma González was born in 1999 in Florida. She went to the Marjory Stoneman Douglas High School and enjoyed studying politics, creative writing, and astronomy. Emma was a bright-eyed, happy student, with lots of close friends, interests, and hobbies.

Then, on February 14, 2018, her life took a shocking turn. A young man with a gun walked into Emma's school and started shooting at people. It was a terrifying ordeal, and, at the time, nobody really understood what was going on. It was only days later that Emma discovered the extent of the tragedy—seventeen of her teachers and fellow students had been killed.

> **TEACHERS DO NOT NEED TO BE ARMED WITH GUNS TO PROTECT THEIR CLASSES. THEY NEED TO BE ARMED WITH A SOLID EDUCATION. . . .**

CHALLENGING THE LAWMAKERS

In America, it's not against the law for people to b guns and, sadly, school shootings are not so unusu Many people campaign for the laws to be change They think it should be much harder for people to buy weapons. But guns are big business in Americ and the companies that make and sell them, led by the National Rifle Association, the NRA, are very powerful. Many politicians support the NRA and, i return, the NRA donates money to these politicians This all means that it's very, very difficult to persua the politicians to change the laws.

Emma desperately wanted things to change. She knew that if she didn't challenge the system somehow, there would be more school shootings in the future. So, along with other pupils from her school, she joined a movement called Never Agair MSD (Marjory Stoneman Douglas) and began protesting about gun laws.

> **WE ARE TIRED OF BEING IGNORED.**

MARCH FOR OUR LIVES

> **" IF YOU ACTIVELY DO NOTHING, PEOPLE CONTINUALLY END UP DEAD, SO IT'S TIME TO START DOING SOMETHING. "**

Just three days after the shooting, Emma mustered remarkable strength to speak at a gun-control demonstration. She spoke fiercely about leaders not being interested in changing the laws or listening to what young people like her had to say. She demanded that politicians stop taking money from the gun industry and wake up to the fact that children were dying. The way she talked was so heartfelt, she persuaded many people to support her cause. And Emma wasn't afraid to argue with the politicians face-to-face, either. Fed up with being dismissed, she challenged an experienced politician on live television about their support for the NRA.

One month later, on March 24, a March For Our Lives rally was organized across cities in America. Hundreds of thousands of people came out to support a change to the gun laws, and even more people around the world followed the march on television. Emma gave a speech, listing the names of every shooting victim from her school, reminding the crowd of the simple things they would never get to do again. Then she waited in silence until six minutes and twenty seconds had passed—the same amount of time it took for the gunman's attack to come to an end. It was an incredibly moving, powerful speech.

Emma, joined by 800,000 people, speaking at the March For Our Lives protest in 2018, asking American politicians for stricter gun control laws

SHAKING UP THE WORLD

And Emma's campaigning has made a difference. Thanks to her and Never Again MSD, in March 2018, Florida's lawmakers passed a bill—the Marjory Stoneman Douglas High School Public Safety Act—that was designed to make schools safer. And gun laws across the rest of America are slowly beginning to change too.

Emma experienced something truly shocking on that day in February 2018, but through her courage to protest and desire to make a difference, she has helped force a change, and created hope for a better future.

Emma unveiling a Stop Gun Violence mural in New York City

EMMA GONZÁLEZ

105

WHEN THEY WERE BORN

Pocahontas
1596—1617

Blaise Pascal
1623—1662

Wolfgang Amadeus Mozart
1756—1791

Mary Anning
1799—1847

Louis Braille
1809—1852

Clara Schuman
1819—1896

Pablo Picasso
1881—1973

Momčilo Gavrić
1906—1993

Shirley Temple
1928—2014

Anne Frank
1929—1945

Calvin Graham
1930—1992

Claudette Colvi
1939

Pelé
1940

Stevie Wonder
1950

Nadia Comăneci
1961

Hector Pieterson
1963—1976

Björk
1965

Ruth Lawrence
1971

Samantha Smith
1972

Sachin Tendulkar
1973

Wang Yani
1975

Kimmie Weeks
1981

Iqbal Masih
1983—1995

Temba Tsheri
1985

William Kamkwamba
1987

Nkosi Johnson
1989–2001

Mayra Avellar Neves
1990

Bethany Hamilton
1990

Emma Watson
1990

Thandiwe Chama
1991

Michaela Mycroft
1994

Ellie Simmonds
1994

Gulwali Passarlay
1994

Boyan Slat
1994

Laura Dekker
1995

Neha Gupta
1996

Hannah Taylor
1996

Malala Yousafzai
1997

Ann Makosinski
1997

Emma González
1999

Billy Monger
1999

Jordan Casey
2000

Richard Turere
2000

Red Gerard
2000

Skyler Grey
2000

Mohamad Al Jounde
2001

Jade Hameister
2001

Reyhan Jamalova
2002

Greta Thunberg
2003

Marley Dias
2005

GLOSSARY

ACHONDROPLASIA: A condition that causes bones to develop shorter than usual, especially in the arms and legs.

ACTIVIST: A person who campaigns to bring about political or social change.

AIDS: AIDS stands for acquired immune deficiency syndrome. It is a collection of symptoms and illnesses that develop when someone's immune system is damaged after being infected with human immunodeficiency virus, or HIV.

AMBASSADOR: Someone who represents, or works to spread the ideas of, an organization or charity.

AMPUTATION: Surgical removal of all, or part of, an arm or leg. This is usually carried out if the limb is damaged and can't be healed.

APARTHEID: A political system in South Africa where white South Africans forced non-white South Africans (most of the population) to live in separate areas, to use separate public facilities, and to have fewer rights. It was officially law from 1948 to 1991, but in practice ran for much longer.

ARMED FORCES: A country's army, navy, and air force.

BLACK SEA: A large body of water in the southeast of Europe bordered by Ukraine, Russia, Georgia, Turkey, Bulgaria, and Romania.

BRAILLE: A system of writing for blind people, made up of small raised dots that are felt with the fingertips.

CAMPAIGN: A course of action or series of activities that have a particular aim or goal. Campaigns can be military, political, or social.

CEASE-FIRE: A temporary stopping of fighting in a battle, often arranged to allow peace talks to take place, or for civilians to leave the area of fighting safely.

CEREBRAL PALSY: A condition that affects movement and coordination, caused by a problem with the brain that occurs around birth. People with cerebral palsy might have only very mild symptoms or may be affected very severely.

CHOLERA: A name for several different diseases that cause severe and sometimes life-threatening vomiting and diarrhoea.

CITIZEN: A person who lives in a certain region or place, for example, "He was a citizen of the UK."

CONSERVATION: A special effort to protect and preserve something that is valuable, especially nature.

CUBISM: A painting style where artists show solid objects as a series of flat surfaces. Pablo Picasso and Georges Braque were the pioneers of the Cubist Movement in the early twentieth century.

DYNAMO: A machine that turns mechanical energy, or movement, into electrical energy.

FAMINE: A situation in which large numbers of people do not have enough food—often due to war or drought—and many die.

FAVELA: A Brazilian shantytown, or slum, where large numbers of people live in poor housing.

FIRST WORLD WAR: (1914–1918) The war fought between the Central Powers (led by Germany) and the Allied Powers (led by Great Britain, France, Russia, and the United States) for control of Europe, with the Allied Powers winning. Over 16 million people died.

FOSSIL: The remains of a prehistoric plant or animal preserved in rock.

FOSSIL FUEL: A fuel, like coal, oil, or gas, made from the remains of plants and animals that died millions of years ago.

FOSTER PARENTS: Grown-ups who look after a child in their own home, but without becoming the child's legal parents.

GEOMETRY: A kind of math that studies the size, shape, position, and angles of things such as triangles, circles, spheres, or cones.

GEYSER: A hole in the earth's surface through which jets of hot water and steam are regularly forced. The water is heated by molten rock deep in the earth.

GOVERNMENT: A group of people who make decisions about how a country should be run.

GREENHOUSE GASES: Gases—both natural and man-made—that cause the earth's atmosphere to warm up, just as a greenhouse keeps the air inside it warm.

HOLLYWOOD WALK OF FAME: A sidewalk in Hollywood, the home of the film industry, that has over 2,500 stars set into the ground, each one with the name of a person who has been successful in the entertainment industry.

IMMIGRATION: The movement of people from their home country to a foreign country to live permanently.

INTERNATIONAL CHILDREN'S PEACE PRIZE: A prize awarded every year to a child who has done remarkable things to improve the lives of vulnerable children somewhere in the world. Every winner receives an "Nkosi"—a statuette representing a small child pushing a great boulder. The statuette is named after Nkosi Johnson (see page 48).

JOURNALIST: A person who investigates news stories to write about them for newspapers, magazines, or television.

MEMORIAL: A statue or structure built to honor a person or a specific event, or remind people of them.

MOUNT EVEREST: The highest mountain in the world. Part of the Himalayas, on the border between Nepal and China.

MUSKET: A long gun used by soldiers in the sixteenth century.

NATIONAL RIFLE ASSOCIATION: An American organization that campaigns to make sure the use of guns in America is not restricted. It defends the "right to bear arms" or carry a gun, and wants to make it easier to own a gun.

NATIVE AMERICAN: The name sometimes given to the Indigenous groups of people who were living in North and South America before the Europeans arrived.

NAZIS: Followers of the harsh, aggressive political ideas of the Nazi Party, led by Adolf Hitler, which ruled Germany from 1933 to 1945 and started the Second World War. Nazis killed millions of people purely on the basis of their race. They sent Jewish people, the Roma, disabled people, and other minority groups to camps to be murdered during the Holocaust. The Allies—Britain, the US, and the Soviet Union—defeated the Nazis in 1945.

NOBEL PRIZE: Any one of six prizes awarded every year for outstanding work in physics, chemistry, medicine, literature, economics, and the promotion of peace. Funded by the Swedish inventor Alfred Nobel in the late 1800s and given by a panel of Swedish judges (or the Norwegian government for the Peace Prize), the prizes are generally believed to be the world's most prestigious awards.

NUCLEAR MISSILE: An explosive weapon that uses the destructive power of nuclear energy to cause damage. This is generated by either splitting atoms, known as fission, or forcing atoms together, fusion.

ORCHESTRA: A large group of musicians who perform pieces of music together. They play string, brass, woodwind, and percussion instruments and are led by a conductor.

OSCAR: The nickname given to an Academy Award—an award for excellence presented each year by the Academy of Motion Picture Arts and Sciences to people who work in the film industry.

PALEONTOLOGIST: A scientist who studies fossils to understand the earth's past.

PARALYMPIC GAMES: An international competition for athletes with disabilities held in association with the Olympic Games.

PARLIAMENT: A group of people, chosen by the public, who debate the government's plans for a country. A government that has a parliament cannot make new laws without the parliament's agreement.

PHYSICS: An area of science that studies matter and energy.

POLITICIAN: A person who works in politics.

POPE: The leader of the Roman Catholic Church, and bishop of Rome. Always a man, the pope lives in Vatican City, an independent city-state in Rome, Italy.

REFUGEE: A person forced to leave their country to escape war, natural disasters, or cruel treatment from the government.

RENEWABLE ENERGY: Energy generated using natural processes that don't run out, such as wind or solar power.

SECOND WORLD WAR: (1939–1945) The war fought between the Axis Powers (Germany, Italy, and Japan) and the Allied Powers (France, Great Britain, the United States, and Russia). The Allies eventually won the war. Around 50 million people were killed.

SEGREGATION: The practice of keeping certain groups of people apart, often based on race, sex, or religion.

SLAVERY: The system of owning people as if they were goods, and forcing them to work without proper payment, often in poor conditions.

STRIKE: The act of an individual or group refusing to work to protest something, often poor working conditions or pay.

SURREALISM: An art movement of the early twentieth century that ignored logic and reality and instead allowed the creative mind to roam free, often painting totally unconnected images and ideas together.

SYMPHONY: A long piece of classical music written for an orchestra, commonly made up of four sections, or movements.

TALIBAN: An ultraconservative group of Muslim extremists, started in the mid-1990s, which took over Afghanistan and imposed extremely strict rules, especially on women.

TOWNSHIP: A city or suburb of a city in South Africa. During apartheid, townships were where black people, who worked in nearby white-only communities, lived.

UNITED NATIONS: An international group of countries, formed in 1945, that aims to promote peace and security in the world, establish friendly relations between member countries, support human rights, and uphold international law through cooperation and mutual respect.

WHITE HOUSE: The official home, and office, of the president of the US, situated in Washington, DC.

WORLD CUP: A soccer competition, held every four years, where teams from different countries play to become world champions.

INDEX

ACKNOWLEDGMENTS
(Key: b-bottom; c-center; l-left; r-right; t-top)

7 Per Grunditz / Alamy Stock Photo (tr); Liv Oeian / Alamy Stock Photo. 8 Maciej Dakowicz / Alamy Stock Photo (tl). 9 Maciej Dakowicz / Alamy Stock Photo (c); Ida Mae Astute / Contributor (bl). 11 Trinity Mirror / Mirrorpix / Alamy Stock Photo (tl); Oxford Picture Library / Alamy Stock Photo (c). 12 Nigel Cattlin / Alamy Stock Photo (br). 13 Jeffrey Isaac Greenberg 7 / Alamy Stock Photo (tr); Phil Degginger / Alamy Stock Photo (c). 15 Isa Foltin / Contributor (tr); Joern Pollex / Stringer (c). 16 Granger Historical Picture Archive / Alamy Stock Photo (tl). 17 Science History Images / Alamy Stock Photo (bc); The History Collection / Alamy Stock Photo (bl). 19 Brent Stirton / Staff (tr); FLPA / Alamy Stock Photo (tc). 20 All Canada Photos / Alamy Stock Photo (bl); Michel Porro / Contributor (br). 21 MediaNews Group/East Bay Times via Getty Images / Contributor (tr). 22–23 Fabrizio Troiani / Alamy Stock Photo (br). 25 Sebastien Micke/Paris Match / Contributor (tl); Sebastien Micke/Paris Match / Contributor (bl). 26 Trinity Mirror / Mirrorpix / Alamy Stock Photo (br). 27 Pictorial Press Ltd / Alamy Stock Photo (tr); Hayk Shalunts / Alamy Stock Photo (br). 28 PAINTING / Alamy Stock Photo (cl). 29 Granger Historical Picture Archive / Alamy Stock Photo (cl); Science History Images / Alamy Stock Photo (bl). 30 DWD-Media / Alamy Stock Photo (cr); United Archives GmbH / Alamy Stock Phot (bl); Entertainment Pictures / Alamy Stock Photo (cb). 31 roger parkes / Alamy Stock Photo (bl). 32 INTERFOTO / Alamy Stock Photo (bl). 33 age fotostock / Alamy Stock Photo (cr). 34 CBW / Alamy Stock Photo (cr). 35 Steve Granitz / Contributor (br); Nordicphotos / Alamy Stock Photo (bc). 36 Eye Ubiquitous / Alamy Stock Photo (cr); World History Archive / Alamy Stock Photo (br). 39 Heritage Image Partnership Ltd / Alamy Stock Photo (cl); Art Collection 2 / Alamy Stock Photo (bl). 40 Jared Siskin / Stringer (cr); Jared Siskin / Stringer (bl). 41 WENN Rights Ltd / Alamy Stock Photo (cr). 42 Granger Historical Picture Archive / Alamy Stock Photo (bl). 43 Everett Collection, Inc. / Alamy Stock Photo (c); Pictorial Press Ltd / Alamy Stock Photo (cr); travelview / Shutterstock.com (bl). 45 Cynthia Johnson / Contributor (tr); Le Do / Shutterstock.com (br). 46 United Archives GmbH / Alamy Stock Photo (tr); Everett Collection Inc / Alamy Stock Photo (bl). 47 Heritage Image Partnership Ltd / Alamy Stock Photo (tr). 49 RAJESH JANTILAL / Stringer (bl). 51 Gulwali Passarlay (tl); Ken McKay/ITV/Shutterstock (c); Jono Photography / Shutterstock.com (bl). 53 Mike Coppola / Staff (tr); Erin Patrice O'Brien Photography, Inc /Contour / Contributor (bl); Monica Schipper / Stringer (bc). 55 dpa picture alliance / Alamy Stock Photo (cl); CBW / Alamy Stock Photo (bl). 56 History and Art Collection / Alamy Stock Photo (cl). 57 Everett Collection Historical / Alamy Stock Photo (tl); Archive PL / Alamy Stock Photo (br). 59 Michaela Mycroft (tr); Michaela Mycroft (cr); Michaela Mycroft (br). 61 Niday Picture Library / Alamy Stock Photo (tr); Robert Carner / Alamy Stock Photo (cr); Gibson Green / Alamy Stock Photo (bl). 63 Xinhua / Alamy Stock Photo (tr); ROBIN VAN LONKHUIJSEN / Contributor (cl). 64 Hemis / Alamy Stock Photo (tl); Colin McConnell / Contributor (bl). 65 Rick Eglinton / Contributor (br). 66 INTERFOTO / Alamy Stock Photo (cl). 67 Everett Collection Inc / Alamy Stock Photo (c); UtCon Collection / Alamy Stock Photo (c); Chronicle / Alamy Stock Photo (bl). 68 Allstar Picture Library / Alamy Stock Photo (bl); AF archive / Alamy Stock Photo (bc). 70 christopher jones / Alamy Stock Photo (cl). 71 Mark Davidson / Alamy Stock Photo (tr); Feng Li / Staff (bl). 73 James D. Morgan / Contributor (tr). 75 Dinodia Photos / Alamy Stock Photo (tc); Dinodia Photos / Alamy Stock Photo (tr). 77 ZUMA Press, Inc. / Alamy Stock Photo (tl); Sam Mellish / Contributor (cr). 79 ZUMA / Alamy Stock Photo (cl); Katharine Lotze / Staff (bl). 81 John van Hasselt - Corbis / Contributor (cl); Nick Fulford / Alamy Stock Photo (bl). 83 Aflo Co., Ltd. / Alamy Stock Photo (tl); ZUMA / Alamy Stock Photo (cl). 85 Bryn Lennon / Staff (tr); Action Plus Sports Images / Alamy Stock Photo (bl). 87 Three Lions / Stringer (cr); Everett Collection Inc / Alamy Stock Photo (bl). 89 Keystone Press / Alamy Stock Photo (tr); Anadolu Agency / Contributor (cr). 90 ITAR-TASS News Agency / Alamy Stock Photo (bl). 91 ITAR-TASS News Agency / Alamy Stock Photo (tr). 92 Archive PL / Alamy Stock Photo (tl). 94 robertharding / Alamy Stock Photo (cr). 95 John van Hasselt - Corbis / Contributor (tr); Pacific Press Agency / Alamy Stock Photo (cr). 96 Friedrich Stark / Alamy Stock Photo (bc). 98 robertharding / Alamy Stock Photo (cl). 99 Paul Morigi / Contributor (cl); Jake Lyell / Alamy Stock Photo (bl). 100 Jacki Wu / Alamy Stock Photo (tr). 101 ROBIN UTRECHT / Staff (cr). 103 dpa picture alliance / Alamy Stock Photo (cl); Xinhua / Alamy Stock Photo (bl). 105 Pacific Press Agency / Alamy Stock Photo (tl); Noam Galai / Contributor (bl).

CHAPTER EXPLANATIONS

THINK & INVENT

You need an incredible mind to make new discoveries, to dream up fantastic new ideas, and to invent amazing new machines—it's daring, creative, and adventurous. The children in this chapter have all used their intelligence and ingenuity to tackle problems in a totally new way, and their brilliance has made the world a better place for everyone.

CREATE & DREAM

To ignore the rules and create something totally new takes confidence, but also a unique way of seeing the world. The children in this chapter all saw possibilities that no one else saw and had dreams that no one else dreamed, and their innovative view of the world inspired others but also made the world a richer, more beautiful place.

HOPE & BELIEVE

Sometimes, when the world seems against you, when everything you've tried has failed, it's easy to despair. The children in this chapter all faced difficult challenges but refused to give up. They believed their lives could be better and the world could be fairer and, most importantly, they never lost hope. They proved that, with hope and belief in yourself, anything is possible.

LEAD & TRIUMPH

A great leader keeps going till the final whistle and has the strength not just to complete a challenge, but to triumph at it. Great champions are great role models—they inspire and encourage—and the children in this chapter are all leaders in their field and have shown themselves to be worthy winners.

CHANGE & CONQUER

Creating change or overcoming a problem can be tough sometimes. The children in this chapter all came across something they believed was wrong, were strong-minded enough to want to change it, and then acted, no matter what the possible consequences. These children reveal the courage and determination it takes to make a change and conquer.